This is the most flammable goddamn
mess of scenery I ever saw...
Will J. Davis
Iroquois Theater Owner

Mat. DEC. 30.

T CENTER 12

ORCHESTRA

W | MAT. DEC. 30.
| RETAIN THIS CHECK

ONE AFTERNOON AT THE IROQUOIS

HISTORY AND HAUNTINGS OF AMERICA'S DEADLIEST THEATER FIRE

BY TROY TAYLOR

AN AMERICAN HAUNTINGS INK BOOK

ONE AFTERNOON AT THE IROQUOIS:
History and Hauntings of America's Deadliest Theater Fire

© Copyright 2021 by Troy Taylor
All Rights Reserved

ISBN: 978-1-7352706-3-0

Published by American Hauntings Ink
228 South Mauvaisterre Street - Jacksonville IL - 62650
www.americanhauntingsink.com

Publisher's Note:
No part of this publication may be reproduced, distributed, or transmitted in any form or by any means, including photocopying, recording, or other electronic or mechanical methods, without the prior written consent of the publisher, except in the case of brief quotations embodied in critical reviews or other noncommercial uses permitted by copyright law.

Cover Design by April Slaughter
Interior Design by Troy Taylor

Printed in the United States of America

DECEMBER 30, 1903

Dancing! Yes, the pillars of flame danced! To the multitude swept into eternity before the hurricane of flame and the few who were dragged out hideously disfigured and burned almost beyond all semblance of human beings it seemed indeed a dance of death.
Marshall Everett

In his dressing room at the back of the theater, Eddie Foy hurriedly changed into his costume. It was one of his trademark dresses - Eddie almost always appeared in "drag," a term coined in the nineteenth century to describe the petticoats worn by actors playing women - and this costume was no different.

The headliner show that afternoon was *Mr. Bluebeard,* and in it, Eddie played one of seven ugly sisters. Wearing an absurd red wig with a ponytail, he also performed a trick number with a baby elephant -- played by two actors - that he taught to dance. But at this point in the show, he needed to squeeze into tights, a short smock, and a wig to portray the "The Old Woman Who Lived in a Shoe." He would have two songs to belt out when he reached the stage, and they were sure to send the crowd into fits of laughter.

Eddie Foy was a beloved performer, well-known across the Midwest, even if *Mr. Bluebeard* had gotten mixed reviews. The shows during the previous week hadn't sold the tickets that the producers had hoped, and word was out that the troupe would be ending its run in Chicago in early January.

But then, following Christmas, business picked up. On that Wednesday afternoon, the house was packed, and many were standing. As Eddie recalled, "I was struck by the fact that I had never seen so many women and children. Even the gallery was full."

What Eddie couldn't see beyond the bright stage lights was that the auditorium was not merely "full" - it was overflowing. Not only were people standing four deep in the designated areas behind the last row of seats, but many were sitting in the aisles and standing along the walls on both sides of the vast room. One usher estimated that there were at least 500 more people than the theater's capacity allowed.

The show had already been running for nearly two hours. There had been singing, dancing, and even the appearance of the famous Grigolatis - a group of 16 German aerialists who performed in the gridiron - high above the auditorium.

But as Eddie worked his way into his costume, he realized that something didn't sound right on the stage. The audience wasn't laughing anymore. Were those screams? And was that someone shouting "Fire!"? Frightened, he hurried to the door of the dressing room and pulled it open.

"I knew there was something deadly wrong," he later said.

Eddie immediately searched for his young son, Bryan, who had accompanied him to the theater that day. He called his name, and the boy replied. They stumbled toward each other in the darkness. As he picked up Bryan, he heard more terrified voices raising the cry of "Fire!" At that moment, the more than 1,800 people packed into the "absolutely fireproof" Iroquois Theater began to panic.

Some of the audience had risen to their feet. Others were running and climbing over the seats to get to the back of the house and the side exits. As Keith Pickerell of Kenosha, Wisconsin, later recalled, "Men were fighting with women. They tore aside children to push through. They fought like demons."

Eddie Foy grabbed his son and rushed to the stage exit but felt compelled to go back and try and help. He pressed the boy into the arms of a fleeing stagehand and returned to the stage, hoping to calm down the audience and direct the stage's fireproof curtain to come down.

By the time he made it to the edge of the boards, he was alone. The cast had abandoned the stage, and he finally had a full view of the chaos in the theater seats. The backdrop behind him was blazing and burning bits of scenery rained down from above.

Smoke billowed around him as he stepped to the edge of the footlights, still partially clothed in his ridiculous costume.

"Don't get excited," he shouted at the people he could see beyond the footlights. "Sit down! It will be all right! There is no danger, take it easy!"

Remarkably, some of the people in the front rows took their seats again. Even some of the people in the gallery sat back down.

A woman named Josephine Petry had been in the top row, with standees four deep behind her. As she started to leave, she heard Eddie call out. She later said, "Some people said, 'Keep your seats.' I got up, and some beside me said, 'Sit down, there's nothing the matter.'"

From the stage, Annabelle Whitford saw things differently. "The audience was shrinking back in fascinated horror," she said."

Others were running for their lives, leaving behind a trail of coats, scarves, hats, and other belongings as they scrambled to safety. Others remained sitting or standing, frozen in place.

When the performance on stage stopped, the music stopped, too. From the edge of the stage, Eddie urged musical director Herbert Gillea to get some of the remaining musicians to play something. "An overture, Herbert," Eddie cried, "Play, start an overture, play anything. Keep your orchestra up, keep your music going!" Gillea and six of his musicians struck up the chords of an overture from a production called *Sleeping Beauty and the Beast,* and it managed to have a temporary soothing effect on the crowd.

A flaming set crashed down onto the stage a few moments later, and then Foy asked everyone to get up and calmly leave the theater. "Take your time, folks," he pleaded with them. Don't be frightened, go slow, walk out calmly. Take your time."

Then, Eddie dropped his voice to stagehand, who was on the brink of fleeing from the theater himself. He ordered him, "Lower that iron curtain! Drop the fire curtain! For God's sake, does anyone know how this iron curtain is worked?"

Foy heard timbers cracking above his head, and he made one last plea that everyone proceed slowly from the theater, but by now, no one was listening. As he looked out into the auditorium, he later recalled seeing many people on the main floor leaving in an orderly fashion, but what he saw in the balcony and the gallery terrified him. In the upper tiers, he said, people were in a "mad, animal-like stampede."

Lester Linvonston, a young survivor who vividly recalled seeing Eddie Foy standing at the edge of the stage, pleading for calm, was only distracted from the comedian by a macabre sight that appeared above Foy's head.

"Almost alone and in the center of the house," he later said, he watched "a ballet dancer in a gauzy dress suspended by a steel belt from a wire. Her dress had caught fire, and it burned like paper."

The woman dangling at the end of the wire was Nellie Reed, the British star of the aerial ballet. Despite where she found herself when the fire began, Nellie survived the initial blaze, only to die from her burns at Cook County Hospital a few days later.

Nellie Reed was only one of the hundreds of people who died that afternoon in Chicago, but Nellie and many others would never leave the Iroquois Theater.

They all remain here as memories of one of the most heartbreaking tragedies in American history.

1. "ABSOLUTELY FIREPROOF"

The Iroquois Theater - located on Chicago's busy Randolph Street - opened for the first time on Monday, November 23, 1903. Opening night was called "the event of Chicago's century," and city leaders declared the glittering million-dollar showcase as the best theater in the Midwest and one that could rival, if not exceed, anything in New York. Chicago, now America's second city after surpassing Philadelphia in population, would not settle for being second best at anything.

The grand entrance of the Iroquois Theater, located in downtown Chicago on Randolph Street. It was designed to be the most opulent house in the city and, of course, "absolutely fireproof."

For Chicago city officials, burdened by attacks on the immorality of the vice districts, government corruption, and what seemed to be endless labor strikes, the debut of a new theater not only offered a brief respite from daily problems but a symbol of hope for a new century.

The opulent theater was located in the heart of the city's commercial Loop, named for the two-track Union Elevated trains - more than 1,600 a day - that twisted around the downtown district like a serpent. By day, the area was filled with horse-drawn vehicles, pedestrian traffic, and visitors to the new "high rise" office buildings and the stores like Marshall Field, Mandel

Brothers, Carson, Pirie, Scott, and other fabulous merchandise meccas. And, of course, there was the never-ending hustle of the ugly, block-long City Hall and County Building.

Marshall Field's department store in downtown Chicago during the holiday season of 1903

At night, the area was so filled with theaters, hotels, restaurants, saloons, and wine rooms that it was becoming known as the "Rialto of the Midwest."

The announcement of the new theater generated national interest. When the cornerstone was laid on July 28, the *San Francisco Chronicle* had offered a drawing of the Iroquois' main entrance below the headline, "Chicago to Have A Palatial Theatre." Its owners were listed as Will J. Davis and Harry Powers of Chicago and their partners, Klaw and Erlanger of New York and Nixon and Zimmerman of Philadelphia.

Only steps away from where the streets of Dearborn and Randolph intersected, the Iroquois formed a great "L" extending from Randolph to a narrow alley and, in the rear, to Dearborn. The stage occupied the toe of the "L." The building's size was impressive - its frontage covered 61-feet along Randolph and extended 91-feet north to a lot fronting 110-feet on Dearborn. The main entrance on Randolph opened into a huge vestibule, foyer, grand promenade, and staircase, all of it at a sharp right angle to the auditorium and stage. Parallel to the six-story theater - and across a narrow, cobblestone alley - were Northwestern University's schools of law, dentistry, pharmacology, and chemistry. They were in a building that had once been the Tremont House hotel. On the alley side of the theater were the scenery doors and fire escapes, and at the back of the theater was a small stage door that opened into an empty lot.

Sitting between the dark stone Delaware office building on the corner and John Thompson's restaurant, the new theater protruded onto Randolph Street. It was a dream palace in the middle of a block of mundane four-story structures that included stories, offices, a small

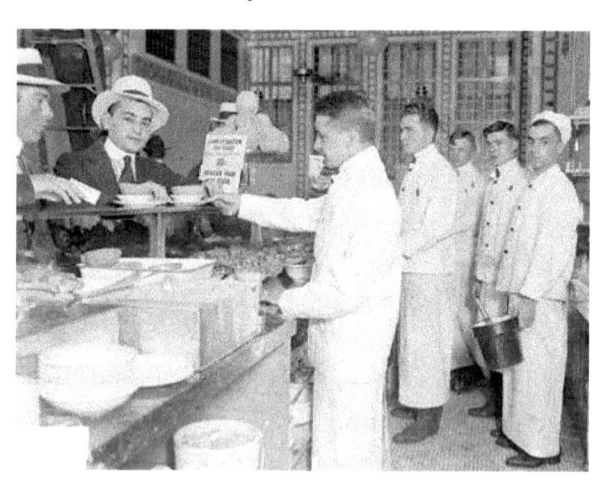

Thompson's Restaurant, next door to the new Iroquois Theater, was one of several locations for the popular cafeteria-style eateries.

hotel, and a bowling alley. Built of steel, brick, and concrete - material that could withstand any fire - the theater and its furnishings represented an investment of $1.1 million, an astronomical sum at a time when $12 a week was a reasonable salary and an average Chicago family lived on about $300 a year.

Obviously, no expense had been spared in building and outfitting the Iroquois. Patterned after the Opera-Comique in Paris, its French-style façade was polished granite and Bedford stone. Massive twin Corinthian columns, each weighing more than 32 tons, framed an entrance with ten glass doors. At the top of the pillars were the epic figures of Comedy and Tragedy, and the entire edifice was crowned with a large stone bust of the theater's namesake Indian, the idea of theater co-owner Will Davis, who owned an extensive collection of Western Americana.

The interior was not only elegant but the epitome of modern technology. At least 2,000 Edison Mazda bulbs burned above and around the grand entry foyer and around the 63,000-square-foot auditorium - a vast chamber arranged so that everyone in the audience, whether in boxes, balcony, or gallery, had an unbroken view of the stage, which was 60-feet wide by 110-feet deep. The stage floor had been designed to be lower than standard so that people in the front rows would have a view from the footlights to the back wall. The auditorium was second in size only to that of the massive Chicago Municipal Auditorium.

The foyer inside the main entrance of the Iroquois

The entrance hall had an ornate 60-foot ceiling, supported by ten columns of marble bracketing a grand promenade. It had white marble walls fitted with large mirrors framed in gold leaf and stone. Ornate chandeliers and illuminated globes in the Beaux-Arts style lighted the arched staircases, bordered with filigreed wrought-iron balustrades that ascended to the box seats and the upper tiers of the theater.

Aside from the walls of gleaming mirrors, the rich dark red of the painted wall panels, and the dull gold of the ceiling, what space remained was covered in what seemed to be miles of red and green plush velvet drapery. The seats in the auditorium were also covered with plush velvet, stuffed with hemp, as were the settees arranged around the promenade and the staircase landings.

High above the auditorium, the theater's dome was circled by a detailed frieze that illustrated the history of theater in Chicago from the early Rice Theatre to the modern Iroquois.

A view of the Iroquois' auditorium, prior to opening night in November 1903

Backstage, out of sight from the audience, the opulence ended. However, there were a variety of modern marvels that astounded the stagehands. There were no fewer than 38 brick-walled dressing rooms rising from the basement on different tiers and able to house 400 performers at a time. This was a practical accommodation in an era when big musical productions often had casts of 300 or more, including young children.

A sizeable electric elevator could whisk actors silently and quickly from their dressing rooms to the stage and stagehands to the very top of the scenery loft. Eleven miles of rope was needed to support the theater's main drop curtains and the approximately 280 heavily painted flats that could be suspended from wooden battens high above the stage. Virtually all the interior and stage lighting was controlled from a large central switchboard just offstage. Its electric cables were safely sheathed in heavy metal conduits.

Interest and excitement over the November 23 opening had been building for months. It did not disappoint those in attendance or even those who watched from the street outside. Police officers directed traffic as carriages, cabs, and even a handful of chauffeur-driven automobiles pulled to the curb and dropped off the city's elite. The elegant men and women emerged from the vehicles in top hats, tuxedos, furs, and the latest Paris fashions. They quickly crossed the pavement under a striped awning to pass through glass and mahogany doors into one of the most elegant venues ever built in the country. It was, as the *Chicago Tribune* called it, "a virtual temple of beauty."

Just five weeks later, it would be a blazing death-trap, but none of that was known on this night.

The audience had come out on this cold November evening to be entertained by a spectacle from London, featuring a Chicago native son, Eddie Foy, one of the leading comedians of the day, and a cast of hundreds.

Many of the city's most influential people were in attendance, including John G. Shedd, who would later head the Marshall Field department store and endow Chicago with a magnificent aquarium. Marketing genius Alexander Revell also passed through the lobby. He was one of the city's

Souvenir booklet from opening night at the Iroquois and the first time that Chicago would see *Mr. Bluebeard*

biggest advertisers and attracted hundreds of customers to his furniture mart each day because of the fully furnished cottage he had set up on its fifth floor. Occupying boxes that night were brothers George and Charles Plamondon, owners of a large machinery plant. R. Hall McCormick, from the McCormick Reaper family, was also there. He, like the others, had recently participated in a highly publicized auction where box seats for the opening night had sold for as much as $225.

Before the show began, the theater's architect, handsome, 29-year-old Benjamin H. Marshall, from one of the oldest

Iroquois Theater architect Benjamin Marshall

families in Chicago, sat with his parents and friends in a $200 box seat and listened to Will Davis deliver a rousing speech that was interrupted often by cheers and applause. Davis credited the embarrassed young architect - as well as Chicago firms and workers - for getting the theater completed in just five months and for building it to the highest standards of safety.

Marshall had studied in Paris and designed other theaters, so he knew that Chicago, still trying to forget about the fire that had nearly wiped out the entire city three decades before, put a high premium on safety. In every public statement, Marshall had emphasized the fact that he had carefully studied every other theater disaster in history so that he could avoid errors in the design of his new building. He wanted to assure the public that the Iroquois was safe.

In the unlikely event that an emergency should arise, he said, the Iroquois could be emptied in less than five minutes if all 30 of the exits were used. The stage was also fitted with an asbestos curtain that could be quickly lowered to protect the audience.

Marshall's message was reinforced to every patron who entered the theater on opening night. In the upper right corner of each playbill that had been handed out to audience members was a statement in bold, black type that stressed the fact that the Iroquois was "Absolutely Fireproof."

It was a claim that would have been challenged had anyone seen the report that appeared in an obscure Chicago trade journal months earlier. Apparently, no one had paid attention to an investigative piece that appeared in the August issue of *Fireproof Magazine*. Its editor, William Clendennin, had inspected the Iroquois while it was still under construction and had noted the "absence of an intake, or stage draft shaft; the exposed reinforcement of the concrete arch above the stage; the presence of wood trim on everything; and the inadequate provision of exits."

And this wasn't the only indication of trouble ahead.

In an early November report to Mayor Carter Harrison, Jr. and the city council, the building commissioner said that of all the city's theaters, only the Municipal Auditorium met all the safety requirements. The structural conditions at the Iroquois were not included in the survey because construction at the theater was still underway, and the commissioner was "certain that the theatre's management would complete all necessary changes and additions before the door opened."

For a city that was growing as quickly as Chicago, the building department was tragically understaffed. There were only 19 inspectors, one fire escape inspector, 11 elevator inspectors, one ironworker, and three clerks. One of whom was responsible for issuing all permits.

There's no record of how many of them could be paid off to look the other way when a permit was needed but based on the corruption that ran rampant in Chicago, it may have been the majority.

The aldermen took the report under advisement, but to spare theater owners substantial added expense, turned the survey back to the mayor, requesting a special committee to study the problem. The issue had effectively been tabled, and the press paid little attention to it.

But that was not the most disturbing warning of danger ahead.

A tour of the Iroquois took place by an officer of the Chicago Fire Department that was never made public. In addition to having no ambulances in 1903, the department had no formal fire prevention bureau. That would not be established until 1911. The closest thing it had to that was a small unit called the Bureau of Explosives, but they had neither the time nor the manpower to make inspections throughout the city. That job was apparently the responsibility of local battalion chiefs.

Days before the official grand opening, the Iroquois was visited by Patrick Jennings, the respected captain of Engine Company 13, located less than a block from the theater. Because the Iroquois was so close, "Paddy" Jennings, as his men called him, dropped by for a routine inspection. He was accompanied by a retired firefighter named William Sallers, who had been hired as the Iroquois house fireman and required to be in house for each performance.

Jennings was shocked by what was missing from the theater.

By 1903, telephones were no longer a novelty in Chicago, yet the theater had no backstage line. In the auditorium, he found no exit signs and that some of the exits were hidden behind heavy drapes. But it was the absence of precautionary backstage equipment that appalled him the most. All of it was supposed to be installed but had never actually made it into the building. There was no fire alarm system, no sprinkler system, and the standpipes had not been connected. There were no backstage fire buckets, and the number of fire hoses was totally inadequate. The only firefighting equipment were six thin, two-foot-long metal canisters containing a popular dry chemical product called "Kilfyre." According to the directions on the label, the white powder inside each of the tubes was to be forcibly thrown in a fan-like arc at the base of any flames. The word "forcibly" was emphasized in the directions, as were the words "never sprinkle." The instructions also included a notation that stated the product could be used to control common household chimney blazes.

Jennings demanded to know the reason for the lack of equipment, and Sallers explained that he feared for his job if he raised objections. Besides, he added, the theater's management had been aware of the problem for some time. Sallers admitted that all he had on hand in case of a fire were the six tubes of Kilfyre.

Jennings shook his head. "If this thing starts going, they will lynch you," he said bluntly.

Iroquois Fireman William Sallers – the man that Paddy Jennings said would be "lynched" if the theater ever caught on fire

Jennings reported the findings of his visit to his superior, First Battalion Chief Jack Hannon. "If a fire ever starts on that stage, it will be frightful," he said.

"What can we do about it?" Hannon replied. The theater owners "have a fireman there, and they know all about it."

Jennings' hands were tied. Bucking a superior officer in those days was political suicide, and it meant the end of his career if he did it. He decided to keep the conditions at the theater to himself.

Little did he know that less than two months later, even worse things would be revealed about the fire safety standards of the Iroquois Theater.

After the show on opening night, co-owners Davis and Powers held an informal reception in the theater's resplendent lobby.

The following day, the newspapers sang the praises of the Iroquois - more than they praised the show, *Mr. Bluebeard* - but the *Tribune* did offer an elaborate photo montage of the theater's promenade foyer, of Eddie Foy in one of his zany costumes, and of the lovely young Chicago-born actress, Bonnie Maginn, a female lead. Its feature-length story about the theater described even small details like "a curtain of deep red velour used between scenes, a brilliantly colored autumn landscape and a woodland scene on the fireproof curtain." The Iroquois, it was said, "challenges comparison as to beauty with any in the world."

What was not reported in the newspapers was that both Klaw and Erlanger, who had helped fund the Iroquois, were in severe financial trouble. This led Will Davis to go out of his way to save money anywhere he could, which was why the safety equipment had never been installed. He also found another major item on which he cut expenses - the asbestos safety curtain -- which would soon have dire consequences.

But Marc Klaw and Abraham Erlanger had problems of their own. They were two of the most powerful men in the theatre industry at the time and controlled, along with other partners, the vast Theatrical Trust from their office on South Broadway in New York. The Trust - which was also known as the "Syndicate" - had a virtual monopoly in the

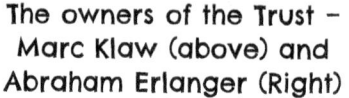

The owners of the Trust – Marc Klaw (above) and Abraham Erlanger (Right)

world of vaudeville and the legitimate stage. Its business practices emulated America's largest companies, which controlled, eliminated, and absorbed competitors and crushed labor opposition.

Created in 1896, the Trust controlled most of the legitimate theaters in the country. Weeks before the opening of the Iroquois, Klaw, and Erlanger had opened the majestic New Amsterdam Theater in Manhattan, which boasted the large stage in New York. It was said to have been "built expressly for musical productions, a monument to the musical's ascendancy to a position of artistic and financial respectability."

But "respectable" was a word never used to describe the Trust. Marc Klaw was a skeletal attorney from Louisville who had worked as both a newspaperman and a press agent. He was described as a "natural diplomate, suave, and easy in his converse with men."

His partner was the exact opposite. Erlanger was a crude little man who had started his theatrical career selling tickets to shows in Cleveland. He was a cruel, mean-spirited bully who kept a bust of Napoleon in his office.

Together, they were the two most feared men in show business. From the start of the Trust, they took over the leases of most of the available first-class theaters in the nation, which gave them an extraordinary amount of power. They soon had the power to decide who and what would play in the theaters under their control. They were ruthless, often demanding, and getting as much as 50-percent of the show's gross profits, after which they demanded commissions from advertising, publicity, booking, and other service fees. If an independent theater owner refused their terms, they would permanently darken his stage, eventually shutting him down by withholding anything but third-rate acts and performers.

Though the two men were unknown to most of the public, Klaw and Erlanger were hated not only by actors and independent theater owners but even by some members of the press who saw them as one more business monopoly that should be destroyed. Even the clergymen disliked them, citing the Trust as responsible for the degradation of American theater and the corruption of Christian morals.

It was easy for the public to dislike Klaw and Erlanger. They were powerful, arrogant, wealthy - and they were Jews.

Among the most outspoken holdouts against the Trust were French actress Sarah Bernhardt and Minnie Madden Fiske, "The First Lady of the American Stage." Her husband, and manager, was Harrison Grey Fiske, the editor, and publisher of New York's *Dramatic Mirror.* In subtle anti-Semitic tones, Fiske wrote about the Trust's "greed, cunning, and inhuman selfishness."

But his innuendoes were mild when compared to what appeared in reviews from *Life's* drama critic, James S. Metcalf. *Life* had been started in 1883 by three Harvard grads as a humor publication with an emphasis on pen-and-ink sketches. In fact, Charles Dana Gibson's "Gibson Girl" illustrations first appeared in its pages. Through Metcalf, the magazine now carried out a crusade against the general tawdriness and commercialism of the American stage and the men who controlled it. While not identified by name at first, there could be no doubt that the attacks were directed at Klaw and Erlanger. At a time when European immigration to America was at its height and Jews by the thousands were fleeing the pogroms in Russia, *Life* was routinely filled with anti-Semitic articles and cartoons. In them, men and women were referred to as "Hebrews," who spoke broken English and were caricatured with large, hooked noses. There were drawings of short, swarthy men with hooked noses luring innocent - presumably Gentile - girls into theaters and similar-looking men in tuxedos and top hats with the caption, "Theatrical Trust. Of the Jews. For the Jews. By the Jews."

In 1904, without mentioning Klaw and Erlanger by name to avoid a libel suit, Metcalf told his readers, "They are not Jews of the better class, certainly not descendants of the poets, prophets, and mighty warriors of Israel. In their veins runs the blood of Fagin, Shylock, and the moneychangers who were scourged from the temple... The two Jews are well clad and have the toad-like appearance which comes from gross feeding."

And it went on from there - literally, for years.

Even with ugly attacks aside, 1903 had not been a good year for the Trust. Ticket sales, especially in New York, had been down, attributed to hard times on Wall Street. In addition, three brothers, the Shuberts, from Syracuse, had formed the Independent Booking Agency as competition for the Trust. An angry Erlanger had banned negative critics from his theaters, causing a backlash from the press. There was also an endless string of disputes with leading entertainers and producers, who refused to comply with Klaw's and Erlanger's demands.

On top of all that, there was intense stage competition to deal with. In Chicago, drama critics generally agreed that the hit of the 1902 season was the new musical *The Wizard of Oz*, based on local author L. Frank Baum's fantasy book. The hit of 1903, which debuted in Chicago just weeks before the Iroquois opened, was a sweetly sentimental operetta called *Babes in Toyland*. Neither of these were Klaw and Erlanger productions, but the Trust had enjoyed success with family-oriented shows like *Aladdin, or the Wonderful Lamp*, *The Crystal Slipper*, and *Sleeping Beauty and the Beast*, all of which had been imported from London's Drury Lane Theater.

The Trust was determined to produce another crowd-pleaser for the 1903 fall season. They had signed Eddie Foy at considerable cost - who was not fond of either Klaw or Erlanger - for $800 per week to star in *Mr. Bluebeard*, which had been a tremendous hit in London.

Even for the wealthy Trust, the cost of the show was staggering. They invested nearly $150,000 in its success, plus $65,000 to ship the sets, lights, costumes, and special effects across the Atlantic. And that cost did not include the expenses for 200 seamstresses and others hired at the last minute so that the show could open in January 1903 at New York's Knickerbocker Theater. These women worked day and night to alter more than 300 costumes to fit the American cast.

But Klaw and Erlanger faced an even more daunting problem than anti-Semitism, competition, declining revenues, growing expenses, and worries that their show would be a hit - labor disputes.

Throughout 1903, Chicago and many other cities were embroiled in a continuous round of labor issues that were so disruptive that it was feared they would significantly affect the Trust's opening of their expensive Midwest investment.

The George A. Fuller construction company was one of a handful of large general contractors in the city that had the men and skill to handle all aspects of general construction. With projects in New York, Boston, Pittsburgh, and other major cities, they had been integral to the Iroquois project. On November 12, less than two weeks before the theater opened, with Fuller's employees' work still incomplete on the roof's ventilation system and exterior fire escapes, bricklayers in New York went on strike at all Fuller projects in that city.

The strike had an immediate effect in every city where Fuller had projects in the works, including Chicago. The strike was settled a few days later, but then Fuller was hit by another, far more serious, walkout. This time it was ironworkers in New York, and while settled quickly, every project across the country had been stalled. When the Iroquois Theater opened for business, it had not yet been completed.

But even before that, the completion of the Iroquois had been delayed when 3,000 Chicago streetcar motormen - who had long been threatening to strike - walked off the job. City officials had warned people in advance that a transit strike was possible, and if it happened, it would seriously tie up all the lines, causing thousands to walk to and from work in the cold, bone-chilling rain that had just settled in over the city.

The strike began on November 14, and, as predicted, caused havoc, making it difficult, if not impossible, for workmen to get to the theater to complete the construction.

News of the delays was not well received in the New York offices of the Theatrical Trust. In the previous summer, Erlanger had been bullying Iroquois co-owners Davis and Powers to speed up construction and get the theater open in time for the fall season - even if it meant giving away free tickets and bribing building officials to look the other way and approve the needed permits. And still, the theater was unfinished. Rumors spread that all the "hustling" that Davis had been doing over the summer was all for nothing.

And those weren't the only rumors. Another story that went around concerned some of the heavily painted *Mr. Bluebeard* scenery flats that were loaded into the theater. Davis was allegedly on hand and threw a fit when he saw them, saying, "that stuff is the most flammable goddam mess of scenery I ever saw! I won't let it go into the theater!" But remembering Erlanger's temper, the Trust's sizable investment in the show, the fact that they owned a percentage of the theater, and that the *Bluebeard* opening could not be indefinitely delayed, Davis relented. "All right, we'll try and get along with the damn stuff," he reportedly said. The scenery went inside.

With everything going on in Chicago at the time, that rumor was ignored.

The Chicago Trolley Strike occurred just around the same time that the Iroquois was opening for business, putting a damper on the celebration

In November 1903, the press and the public were focused on the transit strike - and the possible violence that might go along with it. In a city with a dark history of labor violence, from the Haymarket bombing to the Pullman Strikes, the transit strike was as nasty as it could get short of bloodshed.

Violence had been predicted from the start because of management's decision to keep the cars operating by importing strikebreakers from as far away as St. Louis and New Orleans. Union leaders, though, vowed the vehicles would never leave their barns.

The line was operated under police protection on the first day, and crowds were banned from streets through which the trains passed.

But the following day, November 15, strikers threw large barricades across the tracks, threw stones at the cars, and sliced trolley wires. A piece of military hardware was found in the path of one train - nearly causing a riot because it was mistaken for a bomb - and police began clubbing and arresting the demonstrators. Mayor Harrison was soon under fire for allowing the police to ride, like shotgun guards, on city railway cars.

On the third day of the strike, 500 more uniformed policemen were assigned to patrol the tracks after linemen and repairmen joined the walkout.

Even though peace talks had been announced on the fourth day, shots were fired at police officers and strikebreakers. The police were ordered to board U.S. Mail wagons if the drivers showed any inclination to block the streetcars.

By Saturday, November 22, as contract negotiations were underway, a mob of several thousand men who had gathered to stop food wagons on their way to the car barns charged the police, shouting and throwing rocks. The officers drew their weapons but managed to move the crowd back without a shot being fired. Things didn't go as smoothly on Sunday. Fierce fighting broke out once more between police and strikers. Demonstrators were beaten by the police, and shots were fired over the heads of the mob.

Only one person died during the strike. On the same day that the union was reaching a deal with management, a commuter was accidentally shoved off a crowded platform into the path of an oncoming train.

Chicago's Mayor in 1903, Carter Harrison, Jr.

On November 25, with the intervention of city officials, the strike was ended. The railways reinstated all employees except those proven guilty of violence, and Mayor Harrison spoke for most Chicagoans when he said that the people of the city "had been living in a powder magazine in which men were walking about with lighted matches in their hands."

The tense situation in the city was not good news for the Iroquois. It was bad enough that the transit strike had prevented people, especially women and children, from going into the Loop, but the city was still in a volatile mood after the strike. It was not surprising that attendance for *Mr. Bluebeard* was not what the Trust had been hoping for.

On December 5, the Iroquois reported to New York that "business has been good, but not on the capacity order, which

Just as the Christmas holiday was approaching, temperatures in Chicago plunged to frigid levels, making seasonal shopping bitterly cold in 1903

one might have expected." Eight days later, the story was still the same: "Business has been good but not up to expectations, considering the glories of the production."

Another bit of bad luck followed - the weather turned bad. On December 13, the mercury plunged to 12 below zero, making it the coldest day in Chicago in 36 years. The brutal weather, complicated by yet another transit strike involving over 1,000 Chicago taxi drivers, kept even those who wanted to brave the cold temperatures at home.

But, even so, it was the Christmas season. Parents were going to have to venture out to bring home the wondrous gifts advertised page after page of the newspapers. Toy departments were doing a brisk business in dolls, toy trains, tin soldiers, and in "Teddy" bears, named after the president by an enterprising manufacturer who had seen a cartoon of Roosevelt holding a cub. There were novel new devices for adults like wind-up Columbia phonographs and Kodak Brownie Box cameras and more.

But lost among the headlines, news items, and holiday ads was the fact that Chicago had permitted the opening of a new and wondrous theater - a theater that was dangerously incomplete. And that was a fact known to its managers, owners, architects, builders, ushers, stagehands, performers, building inspectors, and even some fire department members.

It would later turn out that Deputy Building Inspector Edward Loughlin - a 10-year department veteran who had never taken a civil service exam but was responsible for inspecting the Iroquois Theater daily during its construction - issued only a verbal report to his supervisor before the theater's opening.

He said the Iroquois was "completed and OK."

Neither of those things were true.

2. THE SONG AND DANCE MAN

At the turn of the century, American entertainment was undergoing a significant change, primarily because of new technology and inventions but also because of the public's rejection of the old Victorian ideas of propriety. Vaudeville, peep shows, nickelodeons, ragtime, jazz, burlesque, dime museums, and records had become - or were about to become - part of the new lexicon of American amusement and entertainment.

The double-sided phonograph record was about to be introduced. Enrico Caruso, John Phillips Sousa, and Scott Joplin were becoming household names. Popular songs included "In the Good Old Summertime," "My Old Kentucky Home," "Hiawatha," and "The Beer that Made Milwaukee Famous."

The first known silent film version of *Alice in Wonderland* had been released. "Buffalo Bill" Cody was attracting large crowds throughout Europe with his touring company of the Wild West Show. The highlight of which was an Indian attack on a stagecoach whose occupants were saved by the arrival of the U.S. Cavalry with their guns blazing. Minstrel shows were all the rage, featuring white performers in black face who told jokes and mocked African Americans with racist song and dance.

More than 25-percent of the stage productions in cities like Chicago and New York in 1903 were musicals. Many of them were billed as musical comedies. Several held special appeal for children, which is why the Theatrical Trust decided that *Mr. Bluebeard* was the perfect show to open its new Chicago showplace.

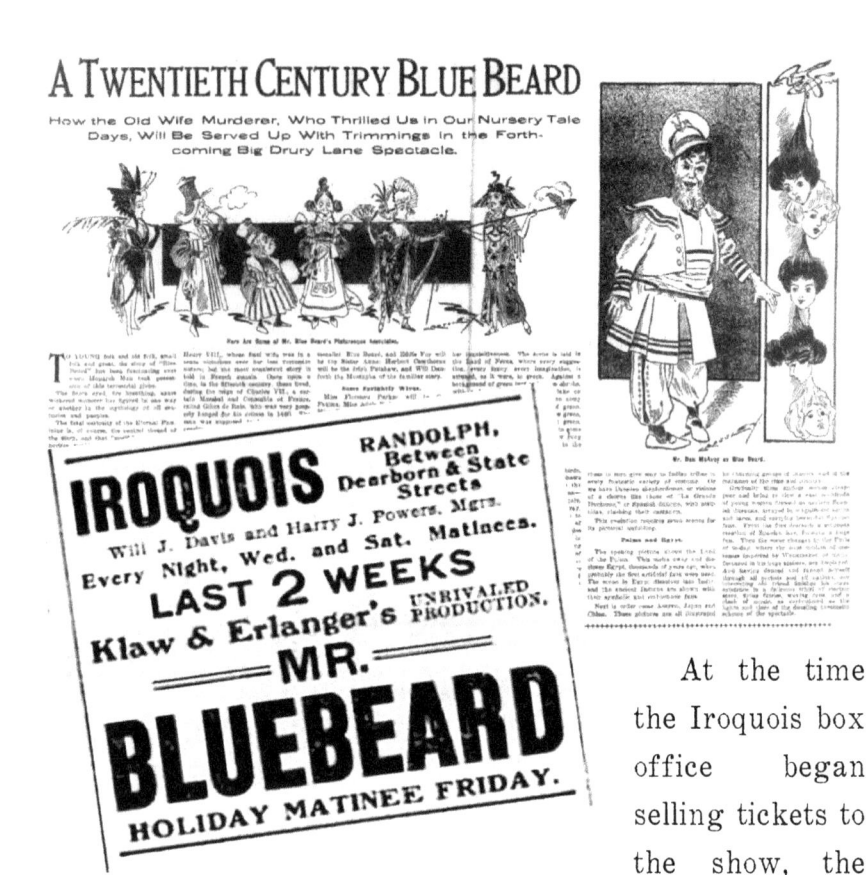

At the time the Iroquois box office began selling tickets to the show, the city's other 36 theaters and music halls were presenting everything from Shakespeare to the aforementioned minstrel shows. It was claimed that more musicals originated in Chicago than any other city outside New York, largely because of the efforts of producer Joseph Howard who created both *The Wizard of Oz* and *Babes in Toyland*.

A show like *Mr. Bluebeard* was something new. It was the precursor to the modern American musical, combining comedy, song, and dance loosely around a storyline and presented by a huge cast of mostly young women and - before the enactment of child labor laws - children.

The new musical comedies were incredibly expensive. Advertisements for *Mr. Bluebeard* boasted of a cast of 400, but that number included not only actors, dancers, and musicians but also stagehands, carpenters, fly men, electricians, wardrobe mistresses, and others. The cost of the show's second act alone was estimated to be over $38,000, and *Bluebeard* was presented in three acts. There were almost 200 people on stage in a wedding scene, most of them in shining armor. Klaw and Erlanger had leased the costumes, scenery, and special effects from the Theatre Royal, Drury Lane Company of London, with the stipulation that it was all for "temporary use" only. Everything was to be returned at the end of the U.S. run of shows - or that was the plan anyway.

Some cast members were from England - notably the charming, flirtatious teenagers in the "Pony Ballet" and Nellie Reed, a pretty young aerial ballerina. She singlehandedly stopped every performance when she flew from the stage toward the dome of the auditorium over the heads of the astonished audience, showering them with paper carnations as she was pulled along by a nearly invisible wire beneath her costume. Nellie's flying act was highlighted in all the largest newspaper ads for the show, and there was no doubt that she amazed the audiences who got to see her.

Nellie Reed, the star of the show's aerial ballet. The death of the pretty young women would become one of the greatest mysteries linked to the fire

There are many contradictory accounts about Nellie's life - and her death, as we'll see later - and little has been recorded about her. When she died, she was believed to be between 17 and 21-years-old. She had come to the United States for the first time in 1901 as a member of the Grigolatis aerialist group and performed in Klaw and Erlanger's *Sleeping Beauty and the Beast*. In an interview with a newspaper in Waterbury, Connecticut, she said she joined the troupe at the age of 15, making her 17 at the time of the fire. Her manager, Hermann Schultze, however, stated that she was 21. She was survived - maybe - by her parents and two older sisters.

Regardless of who she was, Nellie Reed was a much-celebrated member of the company, and her pretty face in the show's advertisements probably sold more tickets than even the presence of Eddie Foy.

And something needed to sell tickets because, despite all the amazing special effects, the critics quickly announced how weak *Mr. Bluebeard* was when it came to storyline and song.

Just weeks before the Iroquois had opened, Chicago audiences had been treated to Victor Herbert's *Babes in Toyland*, a colorful fantasy filled with appealing tunes, including some that are still performed today.

But no one was saying that about *Mr. Bluebeard*.

While the critics praised Foy and the production numbers, the general consensus was this was no *Babes in Toyland*. It was a very loose interpretation of the European fairy tale in which Bluebeard, a rich and cunning monster, marries a young girl and forbids her to enter a specific room in his castle. She disobeys him and, inside the room, she finds the murdered corpses of his previous wives. In some versions of the story, Bluebeard plans to kill her too, but her brothers come to her rescue.

The adaptation created for the Drury Lane in London turned the fairy tale into a bland musical comedy. New characters were added to make it more appealing to American tastes.

It didn't really help.

It also didn't add to the show's quality by moving the setting from Europe to the exotic Far East, with Bluebeard wanting to marry a beauty named Fatima. The queen of the fairies saves the heroine from the fate of Bluebeard's other wives, and Fatima and her true love live happily ever after.

Chicago vaudeville comedian Harry Gilfoil played Bluebeard. He turned a cruel villain into a crooner of comic nonsense songs and an impressionist that made strange noises with his mouth, which was one of Gilfoil's specialties. The queen of the fairies, named Stella for some reason, was played by future Ziegfeld Follies girl Annabelle Whitford, who, wearing a long blue gown, spent much of her time thwarting Bluebeard's schemes. Lovely Chicago actress Bonnie Maginn danced on and off the stage during the show as Ima Dasher, an aptly named character that required at least 12 costume changes.

Another of the stars of *Mr. Bluebeard* was future Ziegfeld Follies performer Annabelle Whitford

Fatima had seven ugly sisters in the show, and the most hideous of them was Anne, played by Eddie Foy in drag. Wearing a dress during a show was a trademark of his, and he had perfected a movement in which he could twist his torso so that he went one way, and the bustle of his dress went flying in another. It never failed to draw laughter from the crowd.

Eddie Foy was the saving grace of *Mr. Bluebeard*, either because he was so genuinely funny, or he just seemed that way because the rest of the show fell so flat. Based on his reviews both before and after this show, I would hazard a guess to say that Eddie was bigger and better than the material he was working with.

Eddie Foy was born Edward Fitzgerald, the son of an Irish immigrant tailor, in the slums of Greenwich Village in lower Manhattan in 1856. After his father's death six years later, he moved with his mother and two siblings to Chicago on the advice of a relative, who mistakenly thought it might be easier to make a living there.

Later in life, Eddie boasted that he could dance from the day he was born. He did start making money as a street performer when he was eight years old, doing Irish dances and acrobatics for pocket change that helped support his family. At age 12, he quit school and hawked newspapers on street corners. Then, when he was 16, he became a professional performer and put together a song-and-dance routine with a friend that got him jobs in local saloons. At first, they billed themselves as "Finnegan and Fitzgerald," but thinking it sounds too Irish, they changed the name to "Edwards and Foy."

Unable to afford even the cheapest tickets to shows, Eddy frequently loitered behind concert halls and wine rooms to hear the minstrel and vaudeville shows inside. On one occasion, when he had enough money for a balcony seat at a minstrel show, he was so impressed with the songs, dancing, and comedy routines that he later referred to that night as "one of the red-letter evenings of my career."

The star performer and the man credited with saving the lives of many in the audience on December 30, 1903, Eddie Foy

There was also another vivid memory from his early days that stuck with him throughout this life - although this one, he likely would have rather forgotten. On October 8, 1871, he was in the city when the Great Chicago Fire reduced a large part of the city to ashes.

Like the O'Learys who were blamed for the fire, the Fitzgerald family lived in the West Side Irish neighborhood in a wooden shack that was destroyed by the inferno. Eddie, who was 15, was told to take his sister's eighteen-month-old son and get out of the area as fast as he could. The family planned to meet again somewhere after the danger had passed. He hurried off to the home of a friend who lived in a part of the city that he believed would be safe because to get to this friend's house, the fire would have to pass through Chicago's central business district, where most of the buildings were considered "fireproof."

It turned out; they weren't. Fanned by strong winds, the fire spread quickly and was soon out of control. Eddie attempted to escape across the Chicago River with his little nephew in his arms, but the narrow wooden bridges were blocked by wagons, carriages, trucks, and terrified pedestrians. Eddie survived the fire like thousands of others by fleeing to the Lake Michigan shoreline and watching helplessly as flames consumed the city. For days after, he and the baby took short napes in church pews and ate what they could at emergency shelters. Finally, he and his nephew found the rest of the family. All of them had survived.

Eddie continued in show business, becoming famous in the later 1870s as a performer in mining camps and cow towns across the West. During this time, he even became friendly with Doc Holliday in Dodge City, where one night he became involved in an altercation over a girl with a fellow actor, who drunkenly shot at Eddie. The gunfire awakened city constable Wyatt Earp, who disarmed the actor and sent both the players home to sleep it off. Foy is also reported to have been in Tombstone, Arizona, in October 1881, appearing at the local theatre when the legendary Gunfight at the OK Corral took place.

In 1886, Eddie married Lola Sefton, who died ten years later, and in 1888 he returned to Chicago. By this time, he was a star comedian on the vaudeville circuit. He played variety shows for years, doing song and dance acts, eventually rising to musical comedy stardom in Broadway hits like *The Strollers* and *Mr. Bluebeard*. Eddie specialized in eccentric routines and costumes, wearing women's clothing to hilarious effect. With his upper lip extended well below his teeth, giving him an unusual V-shaped grin, he usually spoke in a slurred lisp that audiences loved.

In 1896, Foy married Madeline Morando, and in time, they had 11 children together, seven of whom survived into adulthood. Several of them went into show business after playing for years in a vaudeville act that their father created called "Eddie Foy and The Seven Little Foys." They toured successfully for years and even appeared in one motion picture.

In 1903, though, newspapers and critics praised Eddie Foy, knowing that he could elevate the material in *Mr. Bluebeard*. As one writer noted, Eddie Foy was "an active little man with an impressive face who could at once compel a Chicago audience to laughter at the turn of a finger or a wink of the eye."

He undoubtedly was - along with the spectacular special effects - the best thing about the new show. It was claptrap, they said, with lots of glitter and very little else. Reviews in New York were some of the kindest, but even they pointed out that *Mr. Bluebeard* combined gaudiness and noise and crowded them together "in affluent juxtaposition."

When the show began its road tour to Chicago, Eddie received rave reviews. But critics noted that all they could recall about the rest of the show was "a bewildering mass of beautifully blended color; unique and gorgeous costumes, an endless array of sparkling lights, flashing jewels, pretty girls, handsome scenery, merry twinkling feet in a mass of dancing, and over it all a wealth of music, none of it startlingly original, perhaps, but all tuneful, pretty, and fitting. There is practically no story. The well-known fairy tale is barely hinted at, and the plot is the thinnest thread on which a spectacular entertainment can be hung. In short, the piece has no consistency as a story, it is merely a great big spectacular show - a thing of beauty, and it does not pretend to be anything else."

When the production finally made its long-delayed opening in Chicago, some of the city's newspapers expressed disappointment - to say the least. The *Evening Post* hated everything about it, except for Eddie Foy and the show's quick costume changes. The critic there saved his most cutting remarks for local actress Bonnie Maginn, the show's lead dancer. She was, the writer said, "more or less deplorable."

The *Chicago American* was no less kind. "The principals were principals in name only. There was so much chorus and so little principal that the main impression the audience carried away was that *Mr. Bluebeard* could have gone along fairly well even if Mr. Foy had stayed at home and if all the other principals had been indisposed."

The critic from the *Tribune*, W.L. Hubbard, praised the theater but disliked the show. He wrote, "Of story there is little or none and the music of the piece is hopelessly common, save bits here and there which are filched from the classics.

But for most of the audiences who came to see the show - predominantly women and children for afternoon matinees - it didn't matter what the critics wrote or whether the puns failed to arouse the public's enthusiasm. For them, there was only excitement and anticipation. Eddie Foy's reputation alone was enough to guarantee a hilarious show, and the glitter and glitz of the musical numbers was the icing on the cake.

It was a day at the theater - what could go wrong?

3. A COLD CHICAGO AFTERNOON

The morning of Wednesday, December 30, dawned clear and very cold in Chicago. There was a hint of snow in the air, and a biting wind was blowing in from the lake. The temperature would get even colder before the day was over, making it particularly harsh for those forced to walk home from work because of the ongoing livery drivers' strike.

Even early that morning, excitement was building for many of those who would be attending the afternoon matinee of *Mr. Bluebeard*. Hundreds of people would be at the Iroquois that day. Many would never leave it, but many others would survive. Those who witnessed that horror on December 30 - and lived to tell the story - will become part of our account in the pages ahead.

Dorsha Hayes was only a little girl in 1903. She lived in the small town of Galesburg, Illinois, which is about 100 miles west of Chicago and, interestingly, is the hometown of George Washington Gale Ferris, Jr., who created the first Ferris Wheel for the 1893 World's Columbian Exposition in Chicago.

On December 30, Dorsha and her older brother could talk of nothing but the day they were going to spend in the city. Starting with a train ride, visiting the department stores in the Loop, having lunch with their mother and father, and, finally, attending *Mr. Bluebeard* in the new Iroquois Theater.

It would be the first time in any theater for Dorsha, the youngest child in the Hayes family.

Caroline Ludwig, a pretty, 14-year-old Chicago girl whose father was Harry Ludwig, manager of the Hallwood Cash Register Company, was also attending the show that day with her parents and her 18-year-old sister, Eugenie. Her father, whose office was near the Iroquois, had decided to take the day off and spend the afternoon with the family.

Not everyone who worked was as lucky as Harry Ludwig. For most, it was an ordinary workday. Work duties prevented Arthur Hull from attending the afternoon show, but he had arranged it as a surprise for his children. His wife, Marianne, accompanied by the family's maid, Mary Forbes, would take their 12-year-old daughter, Helen, to the Iroquois, along with their two recently adopted sons, Donald, 8, and Dwight, 6.

John R. Thompson had the same predicament. He was the owner of eight restaurants in Chicago, all located throughout the downtown area. One of them was located on Randolph, right next door to the Iroquois. It was a location that he knew had the potential for great profits.

Thompson planned to work that day while his wife remained at home with the maid and their youngest child to prepare a big family supper, but he had purchased matinee tickets in advance for the rest of the family. The party included his daughter Ruthie, 8, her brother, John, Jr., 9, their aunts, Dottie and Alice, and his wife's 80-year-old father, George Holloway, who had come to the city to spend the holidays with the family. Holloway, a devout Quaker, had never been in a theater before - he believed it to be the domain of the Devil - and neither had Ruthie or John, but all were excited about going. Together with their mother and aunts, the younger children had begged their grandfather to go with them, and, against his better judgment, he agreed.

Businessman Charles Plamondon, who attended the opening night of the Iroquois with his brother, George, sent his daughter Charlotte to see *Mr. Bluebeard* that day with a group of her friends in what they were calling a "box party."

Margaret Revell, the seven-year-old daughter of housewares merchant Alexander Revell, also went to the Iroquois that afternoon with her friend, Elizabeth Harris. The two young girls were escorted by the Revell maid.

Elson Barnes, an 11-year-old girl from Jacksonville, Illinois, and her friend, Margery Cooper, were in Chicago for the holidays to visit Margery's married sister and her husband, Mr. And Mrs. H.D. Wright.

The holidays had been wonderful, and the weather was so cold and icy the two girls had been skating in the street. On Wednesday, December 30, Elson sent a penny postcard home to her father, Judge Charles A. Barnes, in Jacksonville. On it, she wrote that her sister was "going to take us to see *Bluebeard* this afternoon."

Elson, Margery, and Mrs. Wright had good seats in the fourth row of the first balcony on the south side, near a side stairway, which ran behind the boxes and then down the main floor.

The girls couldn't wait for the show to begin.

The Sherman Hotel in downtown Chicago, where Eddie Foy stayed in later 1903, was only a short walk from the Iroquois

And there were hundreds of other children who were up early that day, bathed and dressed, and excited about a trip to the theater.

And hundreds of them would never make it home.

In what could perhaps be called a "starring role" within these pages, Eddie Foy was obviously also planning to be at the theater that day. He had to be - he was the star of the show. But he was also annoyed on the morning of December 30. He had planned for his wife and children to come to the matinee that afternoon, but the box office had regretfully informed him that it would be impossible because of the large number of ticket holders and those who would wait until the last moment to purchase the few remaining seats or decide to stand at the back of the house.

Since the entire family couldn't come, Eddie decided to bring only Brian, his six-year-old son, to the theater. He would find him a place to watch the show from - perhaps on the far side of the orchestra pit. He didn't know but had no reason to worry about it.

Eddie had lunch with his family in their suite at the Sherman Hotel and prepared to leave for the theater in enough time to get Bryan settled before he had to apply his makeup and get into costume.

The hotel was so close to the theater that Eddie and his son could walk there in three very cold minutes. With the brisk wind off the lake, Eddie guessed that the temperature must be near zero. He and Bryan arrived at the Iroquois less than an hour before curtain time, and Eddie must have noticed the crowd starting to sell outside. Even so, he had no idea that he would be performing that afternoon to one of the largest audiences of women and children of his career.

Officially, the Iroquois seated 1,602 people, with approximately 700 in the expensive "parquet," -- the seats down in front that overlooked the orchestra pit. There were more than 400 seats in the first balcony, probably just under 500 in the steep, upper balcony. There were four lower boxes, each seating six people, and two upper boxes designed to hold four people in each, but the owners had managed to crowd eight chairs into those boxes.

In addition to those who had purchased tickets to the show in advance were the usual late arrivals. Some came to buy tickets for available standing room, while others had guest passes from their connections with the management, contractors, actors, and theater employees. Some were off-duty employees from neighboring theaters. Others had been given tickets by city inspectors who had done favors for the owners of the theater.

Estimates varied, but because the managers wanted to make up for earlier, smaller shows, it's thought there may have been considerably more than 200 standees that afternoon.

An estimated 1,840 people, most of them women and children, were packed into the house by curtain time. This was far beyond capacity. The overflow had people filling the seats and standing four-deep in the aisles.

And then, to add to the numbers, we must count the crowd that filled the backstage area - nearly 400 actors, dancers, stagehands, and crew.

While most of the spectators that day were Chicagoans, some of those in attendance were from as far away as New York and California. At least one was from South America. Most were in town visiting family for the holidays, and an afternoon show seemed the perfect way to enjoy what the city had to offer.

There were several University of Chicago students in the audience. Walter Zeisler, Fred Leaton, and Henry Richardson studied at the Hyde Park campus, while Daisy Livingston, Agnes Chapin, and Gertrude Falkenstein were students at the College of Teachers. Clyde Blair, the handsome captain of the university's track team, was on a double date with teammate Victor Rice and their girlfriends, Marjorie Mason and Anne Hough. They were seated in the seventh row of the balcony, not far from an Ohio Wesleyan student from Buenos Aires, William McLaughlin, who was in town to attend a family wedding. He was the nephew of the president of Chicago's Armour Institute of Technology.

William McLaughlin was a student from Buenos Aires who was in the theater that day

Barbara Reynolds was not alone in having misgivings about attending the theater that day, but she was there with her daughter, her sister, and her sister's two sons. When she took her seat, Barbara looked around the auditorium and, for no apparent reason, said to her sister, "What a death trap!"

Myron Decker, a prosperous Chicago real estate broker, was also uncomfortable. He had come to the show with his wife and daughter but otherwise would not have come. He had a particular phobia about fire and believed that all theaters were dangerous no matter what they claimed. It was a rare occasion when he attended a show but had reluctantly agreed to come to the Iroquois that day.

On the other hand, Harriet Bray, 11, was thrilled to be there that afternoon. She had come from Indiana to see the show with her father. It was a special treat for her - an experience she called "the thrill of a lifetime."

Chicago real estate broker Myron Decker

Attending the theater was a family tradition for Henry Van Ingen, a Kenosha real estate investor, and his wife, Imogen, and their five children - Grace, 23; Edward, 19; Jack, 18; Margaret, 14; and Elizabeth, 9. Their oldest son, Schuyler, who was 25, had to work that afternoon, but he promised to meet them for supper at the Wellington Hotel after the show.

The Cooper brothers, Willis and Charles, were also from Kenosha and in the audience that day. Willis was

Henry Van Ingen, his wife, Imogen, and their five children attended the show that day - none survived

ONE AFTERNOON AT THE IROQUOIS | 59

WILLIS W. COOPER
~1876 - 1903~

CHARLES F. COOPER
~1894 - 1903~

Willis and Charles Cooper – also from Kenosha, Wisconsin – were in the theater that day and were two of the victims of the blaze

active in Wisconsin politics and was general manager of the largest stocking manufacturing plant in the world. His younger brother, Charles, was the firm's manager and head salesman, and the two men had started one of the first profit-sharing plans for employees in the country. During an era of constant labor unrest, it was quite popular with the workers. With a third brother, the Coopers had also founded an undergarment factory that would evolve into Jockey.

With schools dismissed because of Christmas, many Chicago teachers and even some principals were in attendance that day. They were surrounded by so many restless, loud, and excited children that it must not have seemed like much of a vacation from ordinary life.

One of those students was Edith Mizen, a high school junior. She was there against the wishes of her parents, who didn't believe the theater was a place for a proper young lady. But Edith was insistent, and her parents gave in. She was seated among a group of her friends from Theta Pi Zeta in the sixth row of the dress circle.

Behind the last row of seats in the upper reaches of the balcony was seventy-year-old D.W. Dimmick from Apple River, Illinois. He had come to Chicago to "see the sights." Along with three other people in his party, he planned to stand through all three acts of the show.

The only person in the crowd that day that could be considered a celebrity was Charlie Dexter, a professional baseball player who had just left the Boston Red Sox. Two months earlier, he had taken part in the first World Series when Boston defeated Pittsburgh five games to three. Dexter was never considered much of a batter, but he was a respected utility man, playing a significant number of games in both the infield and outfield during the regular season. Dexter was sitting in one of the theater's boxes with friend and former athlete Frank Houseman, who had one of the shortest careers in baseball history. Houseman had pitched one game for Baltimore in 1886, lost it, and permanently left the game. He now ran a successful tavern.

Charles Dexter, who had played for the Boston Red Sox, was the only person in the audience that day who could be considered a celebrity

The clock ticked closer to curtain time. With so many children in the audience, the Iroquois auditorium was filled with a happy buzz.

But not everyone with tickets had arrived yet.

Earlier that day, on a train coming into Chicago from Galesburg, Dorsha Hayes' mother began having second thoughts about attending the show. Her nervousness was apparent to her son, who repeatedly asked if they were still going to go. Assuming his mother was worried that his little sister might get restless, he assured her that he'd make sure that Dorsha behaved.

But that's not what was bothering Mrs. Hayes.

As they grew close to the Chicago station, she experienced something odd - a "heavy feeling, a terrible despondency, and out of it sharp recurring flashes, the quickening of an alarm, don't go!" She wasn't sure why she was feeling this way, but she couldn't shake the unsettling feeling that they should not attend the matinee performance.

At lunch, her husband apologized for not having gotten main floor seats, reached into his jacket, and produced four tickets for balcony seats. Right then, Mrs. Hayes decided. "We're not going," she said. "We can't, we mustn't, not this time."

She refused to change her mind, and the two confused and disappointed children walked around the Loop with their parents that cold afternoon, ending up in Marshall Field's at just about the time the curtain was going up a short distance away at the Iroquois. The Hayes children - along with their father - didn't think that the store's toy department, as impressive as it was, made up for missing *Mr. Bluebeard*.

But their mother's intuition had saved their lives.

They were not the only children disappointed that day. Ten-year-old Warren Toole was also unhappy. The son of former Montana governor Joseph K. Toole, Warren was visiting Chicago with his family. The boy had recently been victim to an unusual string of strange accidents. Four months earlier, ignoring his parents' warnings, he had been playing with a gun, and it accidentally discharged, wounding him. Before he had completely recovered, he fell from a cart and broke his arm. Then, just before Christmas, his pet dog, for no apparent reason, had jumped onto him and had bitten him between the eyes.

On December 30, Warren was stuck in his family's rooms at the Auditorium Hotel - now the Congress - trying to entertain himself. Earlier that day, he had asked his nurse to take him to see *Mr. Bluebeard*. She, in turn, had asked his father, and he agreed that Warren and his brother could attend the show, but only if their mother returned in time from her shopping trip. With the livery strike and the post-Christmas crowds, Mrs. Toole did not make it back to the hotel until long after the performance had started. Warren was heartbroken and spent the day feeling sorry for himself.

Hours later, though, when he knelt to say his prayers, he would thank God for saving his life.

4. THE SECOND ACT

Anticipation in the auditorium mounted as the lights dimmed and the curtain began to open for the first act of *Mr. Bluebeard*.

But the excitement that rippled through the seats was not being felt backstage among most of the cast and crew. There was an edginess that had started earlier in the week after arguments among some of the group. In the 37 days since the show had opened, most of the cast and crew had gotten along well. There was always gossip to share as a bit of diversion from the boredom of dreary hotel rooms and cheap restaurant suppers – including some about the men who owned the show.

The prominent New York producer Daniel Frohman had married one of his leading ladies, Margaret Illington, who was working in a Klaw and Erlanger show. As usual, the two men didn't care about the feelings of their actors and held Margaret to their letter of her contract with them, meaning she had to work to the end of her show's scheduled run with no breaks allowed. The couple were forced to postpone their honeymoon to suit the whims of the Trust.

The gossip backstage also likely included talk about the heartwarming action taken by the entire company of *Babes in Toyland*, who had adopted a week-old infant found abandoned one night in a box seat at the Majestic Theater in New York. The child was taken to Bellevue Hospital, and the cast and crew pledged a portion of their salaries for the baby's support. Reporters commented that it was "great luck" for an infant to be born, or found abandoned, in a theater, citing an incident from the previous year at the Casino Theater, which, at the time, had not been doing much business. After the birth announcement, though, the theater could barely handle the huge crowds that started coming night after night.

By December 30, the cast and crew at the Iroquois probably wished a baby would be born there, too. There was a lot of nervousness about the show. Despite early reports of "good business," the cast was aware that Chicago attendance was well below expectations. Within the past few days, a rumor spread that Klaw and Erlanger planned to disband *Bluebeard* at the end of its Chicago run in early January and replace it with *Ben Hur*.

With this story making the rounds at the height of the holiday season, the news couldn't be much worse, especially for the younger cast members, including the British girls. If the report was accurate, they faced the prospect of being stranded far from home with no work. So far, though, it was only a rumor, and if the crowd at that day's matinee was any indication, then perhaps their fortunes were on the rise.

Eddie Foy himself peered out through the curtains and saw the massive crowd in the auditorium. The theater was not just full - it was bursting at the seams.

The lights slowly dimmed - *Mr. Bluebeard* had begun.

Once the show began - according to standard operating procedure of the theater - most of the doors leading from the gallery and balcony were locked or bolted by the ushers to keep those who were sitting or standing in the upper tiers from sneaking down in the darkness to more expensive seats. The orders from owners Powers and Davis were carried out that afternoon, even though it was obvious that there were no empty seats anywhere.

As the 26-piece orchestra began the show's opening number, the curtain rose to the top of the proscenium arch revealing the colorful scene of a crowded marketplace in Baghdad, where the chorus performed "Come Buy Our

The cast of *Mr. Bluebeard* on stage. The "X" on the left side of the image shows the approximate spot where the fire began

Luscious Fruits." Other - just as forgettable - songs followed, climaxing with the arrival of the villain.

For those few who had trouble following the very thin plot, the playbill offered a scene-by-scene breakdown of the show, sandwiched between multiple pages of advertising.

The plot in Act One was simple. Mustapha schemes to separate Selim from the beautiful Fatima so he can sell her to Bluebeard, who had arrived in the market to buy some slaves. Her sister, Anne - played by Eddie Foy - falls in love with a roguish man named Irish Patshaw. The scene ends with Bluebeard seizing Fatima and taking her away aboard his yacht. The act then concludes with the first of the show's completely unrelated musical numbers, causing the stage to overflow with young women and children in gossamer fairy costumes. It was all fantasy and magic but did nothing to further the storyline. But the audience didn't care - they loved every minute of it.

During the first intermission, those in the expensive sections and boxes retired to the smoking room or went to freshen up, relax on the plush furniture, and mingle on the promenade. Those in the balcony and gallery -- behind the locked and bolted gates -- flowed through the upper promenade and used the restrooms.

By 3:20 p.m., the second act of *Mr. Bluebeard* was underway. During one of the early scenes, Nellie Reed of the aerial ballet was hooked to a thin trolley wire that would send her high above the audience during a musical number called "The Triumph of the Fan."

The sequence was made even more spectacular using hundreds of colored lights. It created a show like nothing audiences had ever seen before. Some of the bulbs were concealed inside two narrow concave metal reflectors on each side of the stage. Called "front lighting," each reflector was mounted on vertical hinges. When not needed, it was supposed to be pivoted by stagehands so that they disappeared into niches on the stage side of the proscenium arch.

For the "Pale Moonlight" number that was about to start, the lights weren't needed, but a member of the stage crew, for some reason, had not retracted the right stage reflector. It was left slightly extended with an edge of it in the path of the curtains. In the usual business of moving scenery, adjusting lights, moving backdrops, and the hundreds of other things that needed to be done, no one noticed the error.

The crew member at the switchboard used a dimmer to reduce all the lights except for the one used for the "Pale Moonlight" number, which featured a romantic song-and-dance routine in front of the painted floral backdrop of Bluebeard's castle garden. The house lights were completely dark, and the stage was bathed in a soft blue glow from one of the backstage carbon arc lamps, a powerful spotlight created by an electric current arcing between two carbon rods. The spotlight was positioned on a narrow metal bridge about 15 feet above the stage and within a foot or so of the theater's drop curtains and the fixed curtain that prevented the audience from seeing into the wings.

The spotlight was operated by William McMullen, a young assistant electrician. It was a bulky piece of equipment with a large metal hood and reflector and could generate temperatures as high as 4,000 degrees Fahrenheit. There were seven other spotlights located backstage, but they were switched off, and only McMullen's was being used to create the dreamy moonlight atmosphere for the scene.

Herbert Dillea, the show's musical director, raised his violin bow to begin one of its most romantic numbers. Soon, the strains of "Let Us Swear It By the Pale Moonlight" filled the hushed theater. Bluebeard's eight wives, pretty young chlorines with shoulder-length hair, wearing long gowns and broad-brimmed feathered hats, entered from the wings

(Left) **The spotlight that caused the fire, on display at the Chicago History Museum.**

(Above) **Spotlight set-up at the Iroquois in 1903**

and moved slowly toward the center of the stage, where they were met by eight dashing soldiers, who had entered the stage from the other side.

At center stage, the soldiers and the maidens joined hands and slowly began dancing toward the footlights, singing their love song.

As the music was swelling and the young performances began their entrances, William McMullen's spotlight began to sputter and spark. A "slight crackling sound" was heard, and then a few inches of orange flame appeared and began to spread out - moving very slowly - along the fringe of the fixed curtain.

Another light operator, W.H. Aldridge, heard no crackling sound but thought he saw a "flash of light, about six inches long, at the place where the 110-volt line connected" to McMullen's spotlight. "As I looked," he added, "a curtain swayed against the flames. In a moment, the loose edges of the canvas were ablaze."

On the stage below, the cast went into an up-tempo song, swearing their love "by the pale moonlight." McMullen tried slapping at the tiny flame with his hands, but the blaze had grown within seconds, consuming the material above his head and beyond his reach. Fire then spread to the heavier curtains, and he shouted up to a man on the catwalk for help.

"Put it out!" he cried, "put it out!"

The fly man also began slapping at the burning material with his hands. "Damn it! I am, I am!" he yelled down to McMullen.

On stage, the soldiers sang, "We love you madly," begging the young women for a kiss. "So, make no noise but come and joy the boys, on condition that the moon is shining bright." The girls responded, "The reason we allow this liberty, is because you wear a smile that says it's right." And together, they all sang, "Let us swear it by the pale moonlight."

The audience was engrossed in the romantic scene onstage while stagehands, grips, and the men on the catwalks frantically pointed up to the flames continuing to spread on both sides of the garden set. A voice from beneath the light bridge urgently called out, "Look at that fire! Can't you see you're on fire up there? Put it out!"

The flames were growing larger and were now out of reach. Black smoke was starting to rise.

"Look at that other curtain!" someone else yelled. "Put it out!"

Chorus leader Gertrude Lawrence was on the Iroquois stage on the day of the fire

Down below, the music continued, silencing the commotion backstage, and few people in the audience realized what was happening. Madeline Dupont, an actress who played one of the maidens, saw "a little bit of flame on the first drop curtain. I was just above the lamp reflecting on the 'Moonlight' girls. I got in my place and the boys came out and sang their lines. Then, going downstage, I saw the flame getting larger."

Daisy Beaute, another of the girls, danced onto the stage, as did the leader of the chlorines, Gertrude Lawrence, who recalled, "I was going to meet my partner when I first saw it, but I went on working as usual, down to the front, and paid no more attention to it because I thought it would soon be out."

She turned out to be tragically wrong.

William Sallers -- the house fireman who had taken a tour of the theater with Patrick Jennings, the captain of Engine Company 13 -- was on his usual rounds to make sure that no one in the cast or crew was smoking. As he made his way up the stairs from the dressing rooms in the basement, he spotted the flames. He immediately grabbed some tubes of Kilfyre from their wall hooks, ran up the vertical stairs of the light bridge, and began frantically tossing powder onto the still-growing fire. The platform was only 18 inches wide, so he had to hold onto a metal rail with one hand as he threw the powder with the other. But it was too late. The flames had spread to the point that the small amount of powder was almost comically ineffectual.

Tubes of Kilfyre were the only firefighting tools available in the Iroquois - they did nothing to stop the inferno

Herbert Cawthorn, who played Irish Patshaw, watched Sallers empty first one tube of powder on the fire and then another and another. It seemed to Cawthorn that the fireman was swinging the tubes too wildly, flinging the ingredients in every direction but at the actual fire. Sallers later explained that if he seemed too excited, it was because a "seasoned fireman had to act in double time, where a fraction of a second counts a lot."

Double time or not, Sallers did nothing to put out the flames. He called loudly for the theater's asbestos curtain to be lowered.

From his position in the wings, Cawthorn could see the actors on stage still singing the "Pale Moonlight" number. He was sure that they had no idea what was happening, but he was wrong.

Jack Strause, who played one of the soldiers, made his entrance, walked four steps, and danced eight, bringing him to the side of his partner, Daisy Williams. They saw the fire at the same time, and, as they went through their steps, Jack felt Daisy's arm stiffen, but she went on dancing as if nothing out of the ordinary was happening.

In the audience, the first of a few observant spectators also realized that something was wrong.

Walter Flentye, of Glenview, Illinois, recalled that the group was still singing on stage when "I noticed a kind of hesitation on the part of the actors, and pretty soon I saw a few sparks begin to come down about the size of a Roman candle."

On stage, Ethyl Wynn continued to sing and dance but could just make out the faint ringing of bells that signaled for the asbestos curtain to come down. As she danced past Daisy and Madeline, Ethyl whispered, "The curtain will fall, the bells have rung."

Moments later, Daisy told Jack that she felt faint. At about the same moment, another soldier, Frank Holland, told his partner, "Don't stop. Something is happening, but don't stop singing or dancing."

In the orchestra pit, the musicians were wondering how soon the curtain would drop. Herbert Dillea, violin in hand, spotted the glow of the fire in the upper reaches of the theater during the second verse of the song. He gave the order for them to play as fast as they could. The tempo picked up but soon faltered as more of the musicians spotted the flames and began to get rattled. Several of them calmly put down their instruments and exited through the orchestra pit door beneath the stage.

Depending on where they were sitting or standing, some audience members saw the fire by simply following the gaze of the actors, who were now looking up. At first, many of them were merely puzzled, but others were becoming alarmed. Most of the children in the front main floor rows remained in their seats, believing that the glow spreading across the upper reaches of the theater was another of the show's magical effects.

Those in the upper gallery who saw the eerie flickering of the flames had no idea at first about what was happening until bits of burning fabric began falling around members of the cast who were still trying to go on with their number. It was becoming evident that some of them had fallen out of step with the music and others seemed to have lost their voices. Like Daisy and one or two of the other chorus girls, most were terribly frightened and felt faint. Lewis Sackett, a doctor from Elgin, Illinois, would later say that seeing those girls remaining there, still dancing in an effort to quiet the audience, was one of the bravest acts he had ever witnessed.

In the gallery, when the elderly Mr. Dimmick heard a boy near him call out, "Fire!" he told him to be quiet. "If you don't look out, you'll start a panic," he told him.

A similar thing happened to Chicago schoolgirl Ruth Michel, who was sitting in the second row of the gallery with three friends when she saw "a man at the side of the stage making motions with his hands. I didn't know whether he was coming in at the wrong time or not, and then I saw a spark come from above the stage. Then another spark fell down and one in our party said, 'We'll get out of here!' and a man rose and said he would knock our heads off if we got out, so we sat there."

Sitting down in front in the parquet were the four Dee children, who had been brought to the theater by their nanny, Mrs. G.H. Erret. Twelve-year-old Willie was the oldest of the children and the first to realize there was trouble. He immediately asked Mrs. Erret to take them out. She hesitated, though - she thought the flames were part of the show. Willie didn't wait. He grabbed his nearest brother by the hand and hurried up the aisle toward the exit.

Backstage, things became more frightening and chaotic. The stage manager, William Carleton, could not be found -- he had gone to the hardware store -- and one of the stagehands, Joe Dougherty, was trying to handle the curtains from near the switchboard. But Dougherty was filling in for the regular curtain man, who was in the hospital and could not remember which drop should be lowered. The asbestos curtain ran on an endless loop of wire-enforced rope, but he wasn't sure which rope controlled what curtain.

High above him, Charles Sweeney, who had been assigned to the first fly gallery, seized a canvas tarp and was slapping at the flames with some of the other men.

"It got out of our reach," Sweeney said. "It went along the border to toward the center and then it blazed all over and I saw there was no possibility of doing anything."

Sweeney dashed up six flights of stairs to a room filled with chorus girls and led them down to a small stage exit. In the rush to escape, most of the girls dropped everything and left the building wearing only flimsy costumes or tights.

The Grigolatis, the female aerial ballet troupe, were in the lines high above the auditorium when the fire started, preparing for their next number

Other men raced downstairs to rescue girls who were in the dressing rooms under the stage.

High above everyone else, in the theater's gridiron, the Grigolatis, the 12 young female aerialists had a horrifying view of the scene. Clouds of thick, black smoke were rising toward them, and blazing pieces of canvas the size of bed sheets were falling on the stage and the footlights.

William Sallers, still above the stage, saw the same thing and knew the theater was doomed.

The Grigolatis had only seconds to act. One of them, Floraline, who was perched some distance away from the others, was suddenly engulfed in flames from a burning piece of scenery. Before the others could reach her, she panicked, lost her grip on the trapeze, and plunged to the stage, 60 feet below. By the time her companions were able to unhook themselves from their harnesses and scramble down some metal scaffolding to the stage, Floraline had vanished. They could only hope that she had been carried to safety.

All but one of the Grigolatis escaped safely from the theater, but in all the confusion, one aerialist was forgotten. Nellie Reed was still attached to her wire and in terrible danger.

In a fifth-tier dressing room, five young female dancers were sitting and talking, oblivious to what was happening - until they heard the cries of "Fire!" One of them, Violet Sidney, twisted her ankle and fell in the hurry to get out. The other girls ran, but Lola Quinlan stopped to help her. She managed to drag Violet down five flights of stairs and across the back of the burning stage to safety. She was severely burned in the process, but she refused to leave her friend behind.

William Sallers, using his bare hands to tear away some of the burning fabric, shouted loudly for someone to lower the fire curtain and "pull the box" - but there was no alarm box. It had never been installed. The flames were spreading rapidly to other scenery flats hanging in the theater's loft. Sallers was working so hard to try and slow the spread of the fire that he didn't notice that both of his hands were

The ruins of the stage after the blaze. The fire simply devoured everything that had been there – flats, scenery, riggings, costumes, everything.

burned and blistered. He could only hear the screams. "The girls were frantic," he later said, "and the men were not much better."

More voices screamed for the asbestos curtain to come down, but nothing happened. Joe Dougherty and others were still confused about which curtains should be lowered, and more time was lost. A stagehand who had been ordered to sound the fire alarm searched as quickly as he could, but, finding nothing, he burst out of the theater and ran as fast as he could through the streets to notify Engine Company 13 of the blaze.

In his dressing room, half changed into his next costume, Eddie Foy heard the commotion and rushed out to see what was going on. As soon as he opened the door, he knew something was terribly wrong. He immediately searched for his young son, crying out, "Bryan! Bryan!" until he found him in the darkness.

As he stumbled toward a stage door with the boy in his arms, he heard terrified voices raising a cry of "Fire!"

And that was when the massive crowd in the Iroquois Theater auditorium began to panic.

5. INFERNO

Many in the audience sat rooted in horror as the flames began to spread across the upper part of the stage. At first, many didn't see the fire or assumed it was part of the show. But then a ripple went through the crowd as small children rose from their seats, pointing upwards at the slowly moving line of flame.

Some of the audience rose to their feet. Others began to run and climb over the seats to get to the back of the house and the side exits. Many of the standees were blocking the aisles and, since the new theater was unfamiliar to them, were unsure about which way to turn. The rush of those escaping soon turned into a mob that was trying to get out the same way they had come in. Their screams and cries were muffled by the music and the show's cast, still singing as the burning scenery fell around them. Terrified families were quickly torn apart from one another.

Eddie Foy ran to the stage exit with his son but felt compelled to go back and try and help. He later recalled, "Something told me that I was selfish - all those women and children out there would be helpless, trodden under foot in a panic. Something told me I ought to go down and see what I ought to do."

He threw Bryan into the arms of a fleeing stagehand and told him to take the boy out of the theater. "When I went back," he said, "my object was to get the curtain down and calm them. My whole thought was, if they get into a panic, they are killed. I paused a moment to watch Bryan running toward the rear doors. Then I turned and ran to the stage, through the octet, still doing their part though the scenery was blazing over them."

When he reached the stage, Daisy Williams, who had at first "braced up," according to her partner, Jack, "did a few more steps and then collapsed." Jack and another of the chorus soldiers carried her away. The other girls began to faint, overcome by fear or by the black smoke that was now swirling around them. The girls fled the stage, helped, or followed by the boys. Frank Holland, panic-stricken, bolted past Eddie Foy, squeezed out the stage exit, and ran down the street to the safety of his hotel.

From the second-tier balcony outside her dressing room, Annabelle Whitford could see what was happening on stage. When the first pieces of flaming scenery fell, she knew she was in great danger. Her costume included an eight-foot train of lacy fabric that would "burn like a cinder." She threw the train over her shoulder and hurried down the iron staircase.

By the time that Eddie made it to the edge of the stage, just behind the footlights, he was alone. The cast had now abandoned the stage, and he finally had a full view of the chaos in the theater seats. The backdrop behind him was burning, and flaming bits of the backdrops were falling around him like smoldering rain.

Smoke billowed around him as he stepped to the edge of the footlights, still partially clothed in his ridiculous costume. "Don't get excited," he shouted at the people he could see beyond the footlights. "Sit down! It will be all right! There is no danger, take it easy!"

Remarkably, some of the people in the front rows took their seats again. Even some of the people in the gallery sat back down.

A woman named Josephine Petry had been in the top row, with standees four deep behind her, started to leave when she heard Eddie call out. She later said, "Some people said,

'Keep your seats.' I got up and some beside me said, 'Sit down, there's nothing the matter.'"

While some people retook their seats, others ran for their lives, leaving behind a trail of coats, scarves, hats, and other belongings as they scrambled to safety. Others remained sitting or standing, frozen in place.

Lester Livingston, an 11-year-old who lived in Hyde Park, watched as Eddie dashed about on stage and caught a piece of blackened paper. He lamely joked about it to anyone within earshot - doing anything to calm people down. It worked on Lester. "I was so interested in watching Foy that I didn't realize what was happening," he said.

When the performance on stage had stopped, the music stopped, too. Many musicians were scrambling to get to safety, knocking over chairs, dropping their instruments, and scrambling over piles of sheet music.

Lester Livingston

From the edge of the stage, Eddie urged musical director Herbert Gillea to get some of the remaining musicians to play something. "An overture, Herbert," Eddie cried, "Play, start an overture, play anything. Keep your orchestra up, keep your music going!" Gillea and six of his musicians struck up the chords of an overture from a production called

Sleeping Beauty and the Beast, and it managed to have a temporary soothing effect on the crowd.

A few moments later, a flaming set crashed down onto the stage, and Foy asked everyone to get up and calmly leave the theater. "Take your time, folks," he pleaded with them. Don't be frightened, go slow, walk out calmly. Take your time."

Then, Eddie dropped his voice to stagehand, who was on the brink of fleeing from the theater himself. He ordered him, "Lower that iron curtain! Drop the fire curtain! For God's sake, does anyone know how this iron curtain is worked?"

Foy heard timbers cracking above his head, and he made one last plea that everyone walk slowly from the theater, but by now, no one was listening. As he looked out into the auditorium, he later recalled seeing many people on the main floor leaving in an orderly fashion, but what he saw in the balcony and the gallery terrified him. In the upper tiers, he said, people were in a "mad, animal-like stampede."

Lester Livingston, who was still watching Eddie Foy standing at the edge of the stage, pleading for calm, was only distracted from the comedian by a macabre sight that appeared above Foy's head.

"Almost alone and in the center of the house," he later said, he watched "a ballet dancer in a gauzy dress suspended by a steel belt from a wire. Her dress had caught fire, and it burned like paper."

The burning figure was Nellie Reed.

Lester ended up surviving the fire that day. A cousin, seated only a few feet away, never made it out.

John R. Thompson's daughter, Ruthie, had she later said, "joined the yelling crowd. I turned back once to grab my aunt's hand and saw the black shapes of people's heads silhouetted against the solid wall of flame that now reached above the proscenium arch into the ceiling. Those flames were like waterfalls, and they came faster than people could move along in the crowd."

Ruthie was swept along by the adults in her group, her feet only occasionally touching the floor. She saw little, she later recalled but heard the screams and shouts of men, women, and children, most of them separated from their families, running blindly for any exit from the theater they could find.

The young girl from Jacksonville who was visiting her sister, Elson Barnes, described the beginning of the fire in a letter she wrote home that evening. "As some of the chorus were singing, the curtain and some of the wings caught fire and great sheets fell to the floor. I thought it was part of the play at first then some of the chorus girls fell in a dead faint and the managers came out and tried to quiet the people and avoid a panic."

Elson, Margery, and Mrs. Wright were more fortunate than many of the hundreds seated in the balcony. They grabbed their things and began to run as soon as they realized what was happening. Elson later wrote, "Well, I grabbed up my things and Margery had hers and was starting to the central stair, but there being a side stairway right next to us and Mrs. Wright went after her while my one object was to get down the side stairway and I don't remember a thing until I reached the first floor. When I reached the central doorway, there was a stampede and people were on top of each other six feet deep. I then remembered Margery and Mrs. Wright and started back but the mob pushed me down and there were three people on top of me. I cried out and a man jerked me by the arms and pulled me out."

When Elson finally made it out to the street, she was able to find her sister and Margery. They found shelter in an office across the street.

"The fire was awful," she wrote to her father in a letter. "I can't half tell you about it in a letter. They carried the dead and dying away in express wagons and anything they could get."

It would later turn out that Elson, Margery, and Mrs. Wright were the only complete group in the first four rows of the balcony to escape from the fire.

Seats in the auditorium after the fire

A boy named August Klimek, who had arrived at the theater late with his mother and cousins, had been so enthralled by the first act in the show that they were still wearing their overcoats when the fire started. "All of the sudden, sparks began to fall from above the curtain and everybody got up," he said. "We were stunned. Eddie Foy came out and tried to compose the crowd. But my mother said, 'Let's go!'"

Although August said that he normally would have wanted to stay to see what happened next, the look in his mother's eye convinced him to flee. She ordered all the children to hold hands, and they ran. He could hear other mothers and children who had been separated calling out to each other, which made him tighten his grip on his cousin's fingers. "We didn't attempt to leave by the door on the ticket stub," he recalled. "We went to the door we came in. That was still open. If we had to get out the door intended for us, we never would have made it because it was locked. And as we left through the open door, I could see people starting to assemble around the locked exit, trying to get it open and pushing against each other. We would never have gotten out alive."

A young girl named Ella Churcher was sitting with her mother and nephew in the fourth row from the front in the gallery. She could see Eddie Foy on the stage gesturing, but she was too far away to hear what he was saying. "I couldn't hear his words," she later stated, "but his motions were to sit down and keep our seats, and so we did until we saw the red curtain come down."

The red curtain - assumed to be the asbestos curtain - finally began to drop. Most of the stage crew had fled the theater, but someone had figured out a way to lower what was thought would be a fireproof shield between the stage and the audience. It began inching its way down a steel cable between two wooden guide tracks. As if in slow motion, it descended, and then, less than 20 feet above the stage, it suddenly stopped. One end was jammed on the light reflector

View from the edge of the stage, looking out into the auditorium after the fire

that had not been properly closed and the other end sagged down to about five feet above the stage. The wooden guide tracks tore apart, and the curtain -- which was supposed to have been reinforced and made stiff by steel rods and wires -- began to billow out over the orchestra pit and the front rows of seats, pushed by the draft coming from an open stage exit that had been used for escape by the cast and crew.

Some stagehands tried to yank down the curtain. John Massoney, a carpenter working as a scene changer, tried to pull it down, but it was too high for him to get a firm grip. The rest of the crew ran for their lives.

The theater's engineer, Robert Murray, also tried to reach the curtain several times, but it was beyond his grasp, too. He came dangerously close to losing his footing and falling off the stage into the orchestra pit. Realizing the curtain was a lost cause, Murray ran down to the basement and told his crew to shut off the steam in the boilers heating the building, bank all of the fires to prevent an explosion, then get out as quickly as they could. Then he helped a group of chorus girls escape from a basement dressing room by pushing them one at a time through a coal chute that led to an alley. One or two of them were wearing street clothes, but the others were clad in their thin costumes or worse, in nothing but undergarments.

After that, Murray said, "I made a trip around the dressing rooms calling, 'Everybody out down here?'"

He then ran back up the stairs to the stage level and found a young woman whose costume and tights were shredded and burned and whose skin was charred and blistered. Nellie Reed had somehow unhooked herself from her wire, but she was seriously injured and in great pain. Murray said that Nellie was "up against the wall, scratching and screaming." The engineer grabbed her and took her out to the street through a basement coal chute, where he handed her to some rescuers.

Murray had not seen Annabelle Whitford, the terrified fairy queen with her long filmy train thrown over her shoulder. She crossed the burning stage, heading for the scenery dock. "The heat was stifling," she said, "the smoke suffocating. In another minute we who were backstage would have been in a panic if the stagehands hadn't broken open the big double scenery doors with a heavy steel trapeze standard."

When the entire stage had become a blazing inferno, the door had been opened. Without that exit, the entire cast might have perished. Opening the doors undoubtedly saved the lives of the cast and crew, but it sealed the fate of the audience in the upper tiers. The contractors who had built the theater not only failed to connect the controls for the roof's ventilating systems at the switchboard but had nailed shut the vents over the stage and left open vents above the auditorium, creating a chimney effect. The blast of cold air that rushed in the scenery doors and caused the curtain to billow out from the stage, instantly mixed with the heated air fueled by the flames, and the result was a huge deadly blowtorch that one fire official later described as a "back draft."

A churning column of smoke and flames burst out from the opening under the curtain, whirled above the orchestra pit and floor seats, and swept into the balcony and gallery under the open roof vents like a fiery cyclone.

Scene changer John Massoney described it as "a great sheet of circular flame going out under the curtain and into the audience."

Eddie Foy narrowly escaped being in the path of the tremendous funnel of flame because he was standing on the side of the stage.

The fireball sucked the oxygen from the air, burning and asphyxiating anyone in the upper tiers who remained in their seats or were trapped in the aisles. It had such force behind it that it blew open any of the doors that were unlocked.

Mrs. James Pinedo, a late arrival to the show who was standing in the aisle to the right of the orchestra pit, had sat down in a vacated seat when people began fleeing the auditorium. "I have never seen an audience who were saner than these women and children," she later said. "They sat perfectly still while those sparks changed into flames. They were perfectly calm. Then I saw the big ball of flame come out from the stage and I thought, 'Now's the time to get out!'"

Moments later, the last of the ropes holding up the scenery flats on the stage gave away with a roar and a collision that literally shook the building. Tons of wood, ropes, sandbags, pipes, pulleys, lights, rigging and more than 280 pieces of scenery crashed to the stage. The force of the fall instantly knocked out the electrical switchboard, and the auditorium was plunged into complete and utter darkness.

An illustration showing the panic inside of the theater after the fire broke out. The horde of people running for the exits – many of which were locked – led to hundreds of deaths

Screaming and wailing adults and children clawed and battled their way toward the exits with only the light of the inferno raging behind them. The aisles became impassable. As the blaze intensified, the auditorium began to fill with heat and smoke. Screams echoed off the walls and ceilings. Mothers and children were wrenched away from each other, knocked to the floor, and were trampled in the panic. Later, when police officers and firefighters removed the dead from the building, they found just as many dead from suffocation as were burned in the fire. One dead woman even bore the mark of a shoe heel on her face.

Dresses, jackets, trousers, and other articles of clothing were ripped to shreds as people tried to get through to the exits and escape the flames and smoke. When the crowd reached the doors, they found many of them locked. The locking mechanisms had been so confusing to the staff that they had not tried to open them before they fled. Other doors couldn't be opened. They had been designed to swing inward rather than outward, and the crush of people prevented those in the front from pulling the doors open.

In desperation, some of those whose clothing had caught fire jumped from the first balcony to the floor below. Many died instantly. Others suffered agonizing deaths from broken backs that were caused by landing on armrests and seat backs.

A brief flash of light illuminated the hellish scene as the jammed "safety curtain" burst into flames. The curtain, it turned out, had not been made from asbestos but some cheaper material that had been chosen by the theater's co-owner, Will Davis, to save money during the construction.

The orchestra had now also fled the scene, and it was Eddie Foy's turn to run. At that moment, he made a fateful decision. He needed to get out of the theater as quickly as possible and first considered following the crowd through the Randolph Street doors. But, wanting to find his son, he changed his mind and made his way through the burning backstage and out of the scenery doors. He would only realize how lucky his decision had been after he learned of the hundreds of victims found crushed inside those doors.

Those seated in the side boxes fared better than others because the fireball that roared out from under the tangled curtain managed to miss them.

The "box party" of young women - which included Charlotte Plamondon - was there with Mrs. Rollin Keyes of Evanston, who had taken the girls to the theater to celebrate the return of Catherine Keyes from college.

Charlotte's sister, Emily Plamondon, later recalled that the group had sat down in their box shortly after the Act One of the performance. "As far as I could see, the house was filled with women and children," Emily said. "It was about quarter to three when one of the young women in the party asked Mrs. Keyes if she did not smell something burning and an instant afterward, a great cloud of smoke spread across the stage and into the body of the house. Immediately, we realized the danger we were in, as did all around us. Instead of a rush to the doors, the audience gazed for a moment at the stage, and as a whole the people appeared very calm, under the circumstances, and as if contemplating how they would escape."

Charlotte Plamondon

As more smoke emerged, stagehands appeared, shouting for people in the audience to stay in their seats. Emily recalled that people stayed still for only a moment and then began making a mad rush for the doors. The older woman tried to keep the girls together, but then the lights went out.

Charlotte Plamondon, with the other "box party" girls, was in a state of panic and confusion. Later, she only vaguely recalled jumping over the railing of the box, being caught in the arms of a man who might have been a theater employee, and being shoved and pushed up the aisle. It was there, she later said, she heard, "a scream of terror I will never forget. Men were shouting and rushing for the entrance, leaping over the prostrate forms of children and women, and carrying others down with them." Behind Charlotte was a sheet of flame that seemed to be growing larger. She found herself jammed against a pillar on a side aisle. "I know I was almost crushed to death," she explained, "but it didn't hurt. Nothing could hurt, with the screaming and the agonized cries of women and children ringing in your ears."

Her sister, Emily, had followed the other girls out of the box. "We plodded through the aisles," she said, "until we came within 10 feet of the main entrance without encountering any violence from the panic-stricken women and children who were fighting for their lives. Then the crush became terrible, and the party realized that it would be impossible to get to the street through that door." Moments later, though, two of the doors - which had been locked - were broken down by the force of the massive crowd, and the "box party" was swept along with the mob onto the sidewalk.

On the street, Charlotte and Emily found each other. Both were bruised and battered but were the only two girls who had escaped with their coats. They did their best to keep the other girls warm on that bitterly cold afternoon, especially those who had almost had their clothing torn off as they tried to get out of the burning theater.

August Klimek had reached the bottom of the stairs and was almost at an exit when the auditorium went dark. When it did, his cousin George stumbled and fell. In reaching down to pull the boy to his feet, August's mother dropped her mink muff. A few minutes later, when they were standing on Randolph Street, shivering as much from the shock as from the cold, his mother said that she wanted to go back and retrieve the muff - she knew where she had dropped it after all.

"We begged her not to go," August remembered, and she finally agreed not to make the attempt. The family stood there on the street, waiting to see what would happen next. "We couldn't hear a sound from inside the theater. It was all quiet."

Backstage at the Iroquois, though, it was bedlam.

Just before the switchboard went dead, a terrified elevator operator named Robert Smith was still at the controls of the backstage lift, making repeated trips up and down to help cast members escape. When the fire had started, he brought down a load of hysterical chorus girls from the first level.

Waiting for the girls on the stage was an electrician named Archie Barnard. As the girls pushed out of the elevator, some were so frightened and confused that they began to run out onto the burning stage. Barnard and some of the other stagehands quickly formed a sort-of human chain to herd, guide, push, pull, and, in some cases, bodily carry the young women to the stage doors.

On his second trip up, Smith, with his hands trembling, ascended to an area so thick with smoke that he couldn't see and could hardly breathe. He found one girl on the sixth level and rescued another batch of chorus girls on the fifth. By the time he made it down with them, Robert noticed that some of Archie's clothing and hair were smoldering. Even so, Archie remained calm and continued to guide the young actresses to safety outside.

Robert's third trip was his last. He worked his way through the smoke to find some women who were so terrified they had to be dragged into the elevator. The lift had been exposed to so much heat that it was starting to burn. With his hands blistering from the heat, he descended with his last carload and steered them safely out of the building. It was only then that he, Archie, and the rest of the human chain fled to safety.

Peter Quinn, the chief special agent for the Atchison, Topeka & Santa Fe Railroad, was returning to his office that afternoon after attending a trial at the Criminal Courts Building. He had just reached the intersection of Dearborn and Randolph Streets when he spotted a man running from the theater's entrance. The man was not wearing a coat or a hat, despite the cold weather. Quinn saw the man collide with several pedestrians before he found a police officer a short distance away. He said something to him quickly, and the policeman dashed away.

Out of curiosity, Quinn followed the coatless man down the street. He turned quickly and was gone. Assuming he'd lost him, Quinn started to leave but then realized there was an alley behind the theater. It was empty, though. The man was gone.

And then Quinn heard the sounds.

There were screams, and they were coming from a nearby stage door, which was open just a crack. He saw the faces of women pressed against the narrow opening, calling for help and trying to get out.

He ordered them to get back, and then, using some small tools that he had in his pocket, Quinn was able to remove the hinges on the door. The door fell in, releasing those trapped behind it. One by one, nearly 100 of the company of *Mr. Bluebeard* rushed out into the alley.

Peter Quinn later said that, at that moment, "We could not realize the awfulness of what had happened."

If it was bedlam backstage at the theater, then it was Hell in the dark auditorium.

Members of the audience who were among the first to reach the exit doors discovered to their shock and horror that the doors were locked, and the staircases were barricaded with metal accordion gates. Some of the ushers who had deserted their posts at the first cry of "Fire!" - as well as those who remained - stubbornly insisted on following the orders of management - they would not, or could not, open the barricades. One of them, named Willard Sayles, said he had been given explicit orders to lock the wooden inner doors to the auditorium once the performance started. He said, "We had not got instructions as to what doors we were to attend to in case of fire. The only time we got instructions was the Sunday before the house opened when we were told to 'get familiar' with the house. There were no fire drills or anything of the kind."

One of the locked wooden doors that ushers could not - or would not - open during the fire. The rule they insisted on following led to the deaths of scores of people

When the fire started, Clyde Blair, the University of Chicago track star, left his overcoat and hat, grabbed his girlfriend Marjorie, and began maneuvering her through the pushing and shoving mob toward an exit. His friends, Victor and Anne, were right behind him. "The crush at the door was terrific," Clyde later said. "Half the double doors into the promenade were fastened. People dashed against the glass, breaking it, and forcing their way through. One woman fell down in the crowd directly in front of me. She looked up and said, 'For God's sake, don't trample me!' I stepped around her, unable to help her up, and the crowd forced me past." Clyde never saw the woman again.

Verna Goss had attended the show that day with her mother; her five-year-old sister, Helen; a family friend, Mrs. Greenwald; and her son, Leroy. In the rush for the door, Verna reached down and snatched her little sister's hand and pulled her along until the mass of people became too much for the younger girl. She then picked up Helen and ran for safety.

When she made it outside, she turned to look for her mother, who Verna assumed was following behind her, but she recognized none of the people who were streaming from the building, coughing, and choking on the thick black smoke.

Verna and Helen were the only members of their party that survived.

Mrs. William Mueller and her two children, Florence, 5, and Barbara, 7, had tickets for seats in the parquet but were only on the way to sit down when the fire started.

"I was not in the theater auditorium," Mrs. Mueller later recalled, "but was only my way to our seats. As I entered the doors, somebody yelled 'Fire!' I looked up and saw the curtain ablaze. Then came the stampede. I picked up my children and ran toward the door. I was caught in the jam, and it seemed that I would fail to reach it."

She was becoming desperate and was determined to save her children, even if she died in the crush. But then rescue came from an unexpected place.

Mrs. Mueller continued. "Some man saw my plight and jumped to my assistance. He picked up Florence and threw her over the heads of the rushing people. She fell upon the pavement but was not badly injured."

Winnie Gallagher, 11-years-old, was sitting in the third row of the orchestra when the fire began. She almost immediately became separated from her mother in the rush for an exit. Thinking quickly, she climbed onto one of the plush seats and, using them like stepping stones, jumped from seat to seat to an exit, managing to stay completely out of the crowded aisles. She was nearly crushed by the mob at the door but somehow made it out of the theater alive.

Winfred Cardona was with three of her friends and sitting in the seventh row of the parquet when the fire broke out.

She first realized something was wrong when one of the chorus girls looked upward and turned pale. "My eyes followed her glance," Winifred said, "and I saw the telltale sparks shooting about through the flies. The singing continued until the blaze broke out."

A few moments later, Eddie Foy appeared and tried to keep everyone calm. She remembered him telling everyone not to worry because the theater was fireproof.

"We obeyed," Winifred continued, "but when we saw the seething mass behind struggling for the door, we rushed from our seats. I became separated from the other girls and had not gone too far before I stumbled over the prostrate body of a woman who was trampled beyond recognition. For an instant, I thought it was all over. Then I felt someone lift me and I knew no more until I revived in the street."

"It was the most awful experience I have ever had," she remembered. "I consider my escape nothing short of miraculous."

Twelve-year-old Willie Dee, who had come to the show with his three siblings and their nurse, Mrs. G.H. Erret, had fled from the theater with his little brother, Samuel, at the first sign of the fire. Left behind had been Allerton's twin, Edward, and a baby sister, Margaret, just two-and-a-half.

Willie had taken Allerton down the stairs from the first balcony, where they had been seated, but could not get the younger boy to move fast enough to keep ahead of the crowd. They were swept along in the crowd of people until they were dumped outside the front doors and separated. Allerton was eventually found in Thompson's restaurant, safe and unharmed. Willie was still looking for his brother when Allerton's identity was learned.

Samuel, Eddie, and baby sister, Margaret, in a photo likely taken in 1902

The other twin, Edward, was killed where he sat. The nurse and the baby succeeded in getting to the first landing but were knocked down and trampled underfoot. They were left with the dead, but hours later, when firefighters were clearing the building, one of them discovered the baby was still alive. A doctor managed to get her breathing, and she was rushed to his home, where he cared for his patients. It turned out to be too late, though. The baby died early the following morning.

Emil Von Plachecki, a 24-year-old engineering student, had been a standee in the gallery, and as the fireball swept out from the stage, everyone started to scream. Emil felt his face burning, describing the sensation as "like breathing a hot blast from a furnace." As he

Emil Von Plachecki – shown here at a later Coroner's Inquest – was badly injured but managed to escape from the fire

ran toward an exit, he found the stairways leading down from the gallery were blocked. He suddenly remembered the bathroom that he had visited before the show. It had no exit, but it did have a skylight. Emil managed to pull himself up, to a height of 17 feet above the floor, by climbing hand over hand on a strong window cord. Gripping the rope in his left hand, he punched his way through the glass skylight - reinforced with wire mesh - and pulled himself onto the theater's roof. He wrapped his bleeding right hand as he waited to be rescued. In moments, he collapsed in exhaustion from his desperate battle. He tried to crawl across the roof to find a ladder to lower back into the bathroom so that others could use it, but he was too weak. When found, he was rushed to a nearby pharmacy so that his burns and his damaged hand could be treated.

James Strong, a clerk for the Chicago Board of Trade, found the doors locked when he tried to escape from the gallery with his family. He managed to smash a glass transom with his fist and climb through it. None of his three family members survived to follow him - they were found later, burned beyond recognition.

"If the doors hadn't been locked, hundreds of persons could have saved their lives," Strong later said.

The passageway, along which James and many of those who died ran to supposed safety, led toward the front of the theater, past the top entrance to the gallery. James had been unable to secure seats, so he was standing at the rear of the

The utility stairway down which James Strong escaped. He managed to climb through the broken window transom but was unable to open the door and save his family.

gallery with his mother, his wife, and his 16-year-old niece. When the fire started, they ran - as they were supposed to do - toward the nearest exit.

"The exit was crowded,' Strong stated, "We ran on down a passage at the side of it, followed by many others. At the end, down a short flight of stairs, was a door. It was locked. In desperation, I threw myself against it. I couldn't budge it. Then, standing on the top step of the little stairway, I smashed the glass above with my fist and crawled through the transom. When I fell on the outside, I heard the screams on the other side and, scrambling to my feet, I tried to open the door, but couldn't. The key was not there. I ran down a stairway to the floor below, where I found a carpenter. I asked him to give me something to break down the door, and he gave me a short board. I ran back with this and began pounding, but the door was too heavy to break."

James hit the door over and over again with all his strength, but the lock held. "I scarcely know what happened afterward. Smoke was pouring over the transom, and I felt myself suffocating. Alone, or with the assistance of the carpenter, I, at last, found myself at the bottom of the stairway opening into the lobby of the theater. From there, I pushed my way into the street."

"Until then," he said, "I didn't know I was burned."

D.W. Dimmick, the older man who had minutes earlier shushed a child in the balcony to prevent a panic, had to feel his way along the wall in the dark after the lights went out. He later recalled that the "whole front of the stage seemed to burst out in one mass of flame. From all over the house came shrieks and cries of 'Fire!' I started at once hugging the wall on the outside of the stairway. As we went down the platform where the first balcony opens, it seemed that people were stacked up like cordwood. There were men, women, and children in the lot. By crowding out to the wall, we managed to squeeze past the mass of people who were writhing on the floor and blocking the entrance. As we got by the mass on the floor, I turned and caught hold of the arms of a woman, pinned down by the weight resting on her feet. I managed to pull her out and I think she got down safely. I tried to rescue a man who was also caught by the feet, but, although I braced myself against the stairs, I was unable to move him."

"I came in from Apple River to see the sights in Chicago," Dimmick sighed. "I have seen all I can stand."

A man named William Corbett risked his life to go back into the balcony during the fire.

Corbett had stopped a young woman from going up the gallery herself. She begged him to save the lives of her two children. He made a dash for the staircase on the right.

"Don't go up there!" a man called, "You'll get hemmed in!"

Corbett groped his way through the darkness, stumbling over bodies on the staircase until he finally reached the gallery entrance.

"There they were," Corbett said afterward. "Positively the most sickening spectacle I ever saw. They were piled in bunches, in all manner of disarray. I grabbed for the topmost body, a girl of about six years old. Catching her by the wrist, I felt the flesh curl under my grasp. I hurried down with the little one, then back again, each time with the body of a child."

Corbett shook his head. "I then realized no good could come of further effort. Everybody was stark dead. I turned away and fled. I never again want to go near that place."

Georgia Swift, who would be badly shaken and bruised during her escape, had been sitting in the orchestra section. She remembered vividly, "When I reached the back of the auditorium, the aisle was choked with people who had fallen. I looked down to avoid stepping on them and as I did, my eyes caught those of a little boy about seven who was on the floor and unable to rise. He had large, brown eyes and was so neat he looked like a little gentleman. He fascinated me. It was all in a second, I know, but as he saw me looking at him, he said, 'Won't you please help me? Please do?' I stooped to raise him if I could. I seized him under the arms and was then knocked over to my knees in the aisle. I struggled to my feet, but the weight of the crowd was such that I could not turn back, and I was carried through the door."

Georgia then added this - something that she undoubtedly said with great sadness. "The little boy was unquestionably trampled to death, and the memory of those eyes will haunt me forever."

6. ENGINE COMPANY 13

By 1903, automobiles were starting to find their way to Chicago. But even so, most people - as well as the city's fire department - still relied on horse-drawn vehicles.

There were 2,790 miles of streets in Chicago at that time, and about 1,200 miles of them were paved with everything from wooden blocks to crushed stone, brick, granite, or asphalt. Asphalt was the smoothest surface, but it was treacherous for horses in the winter.

And then there was the traffic.

There were no lane markers or signal lights, and wagons, horse carts, and cable cars could go no faster than 10 miles per hour. Average traffic speeds were no more than that of a brisk walk, especially in the Loop, where they were few rules for curbside parking. Even the electric streetcars, light carriages, and the new automobiles could barely move at any speed at all.

City working horses had a hard life, often putting in the same 60-hour week as their owners and then spent their nights in filthy stables.

But things were different for the horses of the Chicago Fire Department. Those horses were groomed daily, exercised, well-fed, and houses in stables that were regularly mucked out and cleaned. The department's men loved and respected the powerful animals that pulled the equipment needed to fight the fires.

Engine Company 13, located at 209 North Dearborn Street, was a typical station house. Within its brick walls, the

Engine Co. 13 as it looked in 1903 at the time of the Iroquois Fire

horses, with their names painted above their stalls, were stabled on the ground floor, which meant there was no room for a kitchen. The men who made up the company's single platoon ate at nearby cafes.

Over the stalls, a long flight of stairs led to the second floor, where bales of hay and heavy bags of oats were winched up and swung into the building on a pivoting boom. Next to the loft were the showers and toilets, the men's wooden equipment lockers, and the sleeping quarters, which was a single large room lined with cots.

Captain "Paddy" Jennings had his private quarters in the front. Jack Hannon, the First Battalion Chief, had quarters on the building's third floor.

LaFrance Metropolitan steam pumper, like the used by Engine Company 13 at the Iroquois Fire

In front of the horse stalls were the apparatus floor, the watch officer's desk, and the telegraph alarm system.

Company 13's most prized piece of equipment was the ornate red-and-gold painted, highly polished LaFrance Metropolitan steam pumper. It was stored next to the lighter red hose wagon. The steamer was a massive machine mounted on spoked iron wheels and a crude suspension system. The technology used to keep the pumper ready for action was simple - jutting from the rear were metal connectors that were attached to a long rubber hose that connected to the hot water heater in the basement. The heater was kept burning around the clock and provided a steady stream of hot water so that when the engine rolled out of the station house, a head of steam was already building inside of its huge boiler.

When the alarm gong over the watch desk clanged out a street alarm box number, chains across the horse stalls automatically dropped, and the horses, usually without a verbal command, trotted out to the front of the building and then backed into their assigned positions in front of the engine and hose wagon.

Anything with an automotive engine could not do that.

The men, typically consisting of the captain, a lieutenant, one engineer, and five "pips" or hose men, then came sliding down the brass pole from their sleeping quarters and finished dressing while the company's two drivers got the horses ready to move. Because of its important Loop location near City Hall, Engine 13's horses were likely kept in harness even when stabled.

When any alarm sounded, the engine driver - John Murphy in 1903 - who had been chosen for not only his ability with the horses but also for his knowledge of every street and alleyway in the sector, quickly climbed aboard and strapped himself into the high leather seat above the front wheels. It could be a treacherous place from which to steer.

At the same time, 13's engineer, Mathias Blaney, a man who knew the dimensions of every water main in his district, fired the engine's furnace with wood shavings and kerosene-soaked cotton. Standing on the fuel box on the back of the vehicle, he or another fireman - there was only room for two on the metal step - would hold onto a brass rail with one hand while feeding kindling or coal into the furnace to bring the steam pressure up to top pumping capacity of 1,000 gallons per minute.

As the front doors of the station house swung open, the hose wagon, carrying the pipe men and the hydrant man armed with a heavy wrench, would be the first out of the building. As the steamer pulled away, the coupling that connected the boiler to the hot water snapped apart, and a valve automatically shut off the flow of hot water.

Some firemen were convinced that their horses could recognize alarm box numbers from the strike of the gong, and perhaps they were right because the animals never needed encouragement to charge out with the full company loaded. They raced through the streets with bells and steam whistles clearing the way.

Even though the popular pulps of the day portrayed the fireman's life as one filled with drama and adventure, it could be sometimes dull but always hard and dangerous in real life. Not only because of the perils of the job but also because men might accidentally be thrown from vehicles or crushed beneath the wheels of the equipment. This is the reason why firefighters today are no longer allowed to ride on the backs or sides of trucks.

Each member of Company 13 knew his assignment inside and out. They practiced and drilled until it became second nature. When approaching a fire, a hydrant man leapt from the moving hose wagon holding the end of the uncoiling pipe, sprinted ahead, and, with his wrench, uncapped the nearest hydrant and wrapped the hose around it. This was done before the horses had even been pulled to a halt. The drivers would then lead the horses away, cover them with blankets, and keep them a safe distance from the fire.

The engineer mounted pressure gauges on the boiler and kept the pumps operating, and the fire stoked. If he needed more coal, he blew the steam whistle. Captain Jennings and his lieutenant quickly calculated the number of hose lengths needed and issued the orders to the pipe men.

Battalion Chief Hannon and his driver, Fireman First Class Michael Corrigan, would arrive at the scene independently in the chief's carriage.

Commonly, three engines and two hook and ladder companies were designated to respond to a first alarm. The nearest company was expected to be the first on the scene. In written reports to their superior officers, company captains had to state the order of their arrival and which unit came first to fight the fire or carry out the rescues. Not surprisingly, there was a lot of competition to be the first company on the scene.

Those were how typical fires were handled in downtown Chicago during the early years of the twentieth century but what happened on December 30, 1903, was anything but typical.

On that bitterly cold Wednesday afternoon, Fireman First Class Michael Corrigan, a 10-year veteran of the department, was sitting comfortably inside the warm Engine 13 station house. He was idly looking out the window when suddenly a man ran up, rapped hard on the glass, and began gesturing. Corrigan couldn't hear him over the street noise, and so he raised the window sash.

"What are you saying?" he asked the man.

It only took a few words for Corrigan to understand the situation. He wheeled about and shouted to his boss, Paddy Jennings, "Let 'em out, captain, there's a fire at the Iroquois!"

In less than 90 seconds, Engine 13's heavy steamer, rumbling along behind the hose wagon, pushed out of the station and raced the short distance to the theater. The men, dressed in standard-issue rubber coats, hip boots, mittens, scarves, and leather helmets with their insignia badges on the front, were the first fire company to arrive.

At that point, there was no other fire company.

There was no sign of trouble at the front of the theater, not yet anyway, so the men went around to the alley that ran behind it. They saw black smoke billowing from the stage and scenery doors.

Corrigan arrived a minute or two later, driving Chief Hannon's buggy. As they wove through traffic and approached the busy intersection of Clark and Randolph, Hannon, who had already seen his share of theater fires, decided not to take any chances. He ordered Corrigan to stop the buggy for a moment, and he pulled the alarm at Fire Box 26 in front of the Sherman House. Immediately, fire gongs began to clang at City Hall.

Engine 13 hooked up a hydrant located near the entrance to the alleyway, known as Couch Place. When Corrigan arrived at the spot, he jumped down from the rig and saw "smoke and people coming out the stage door, some with their clothes on fire. False wigs and beards were burning."

As black smoke rolled out into the alley in waves, the firemen with axes and pike poles were hacking away at the Iroquois' lower exit doors and windows, whose iron shutters had been shut tight.

It was now just after 3:30 in the afternoon. For all anyone knew, the fire may have been burning for 10 minutes or more. Other fire units began arriving on Randolph Street, snarling traffic and attracting crowds of the morbidly curious. They pressed forward, trying to see what was going on.

Fire Marshal Musham at the scene outside of the Iroquois. He is the man in the center wearing the fire helmet.

From City Hall, Fire Marshal William Musham was driven to the scene in his carriage. Chief Francis O'Neill was also quickly on his way, and he soon ordered out every available officer in the downtown district, as well as men from the 1st, 3rd, and 5th divisions, to the theater. Six firemen who had been summoned to his office that day for disciplinary action ran toward the Iroquois on foot.

A man named J.B. Evans was driving a wagon on Randolph Street near the theater around the time of the fire. Leaving one of his assistants in charge of the horse and wagon, he made it to the lobby just as survivors had reached the entrance. He said, "People coming out kept wedging in the doorways owing to the terrific pressure of those behind, trying to escape."

Illustration of firemen and volunteers attempting to save as many of the living as they could from the clustering at the front entrance doors

He and several other men began doing what they could to help. "I tried to pull persons out of the center of the jams at the doors, so as to start the throng ahead. Each time we would release a person from the opening, a score of people would be shot through, and then the crowd would jam again," he recalled. "It seems scarcely credible the way people were wedged in the door openings. Sometimes it required the combined strength of several of us to pull them out. The clothing of the women was torn to fragments. One was stripped to her undershirt in the efforts to haul her out."

One of the men working with Evans was likely John Galvin. He had been standing outside at the box office window, buying tickets for a future show, when he saw the center doors of the lobby foyer and outside entrance doors blown open by what he described as a gust of hot air. "I looked into the foyer and saw people running toward the entrance," he later said. "I realized at once what the trouble was and went to the lobby doors and tried to open a door there, but it was locked on the inside. I tried to pacify people from rushing or crowding, but it was no use. There was probably a dozen cleared the door before the crush came."

The hysterical men, women, children pushed through the bottleneck of unlocked doors, their clothing torn and disheveled, and some of it on fire.

John Galvin continued with his account, "The first person to go down was a rather stout woman, who seemed to be free, when somebody stepped on her skirt. She turned to gather up her skirts and she was borne down by the crowd and then they piled on top of each other."

Galvin kicked in some glass door panels and tried to pull people through the openings. "I was expecting a big crush in the vestibule," he said. "I thought there would be a jam on that stair, but nobody came down the stairs. Not a soul. They never lived to reach it."

The "stout lady" that Galvin saw was likely Anna Woodward, who had been seated in the gallery, and when she saw the fire start, she instantly decided that "if there was going to be a panic it would be wise for me to beat it to the street." She weighed more than 180 pounds, which didn't include the more than 30 pounds of winter street clothing that most women wore at the time. She tried to go through an exit door but found it closed. A man standing on the other side of it refused to open it. Later, a boy who rented opera glasses confirmed that ushers refused to unlock the doors, telling patrons to return to their seats.

Anna added, "I was leaving quietly up to this time, but when he refused to allow me to pass our peaceably, I was determined to get out if I had to make all sorts of noise."

Anna was a big woman, and she was admittedly aggressive when she wanted to be. As the music and singing continued on the stage, she was arming herself with her steel-tipped umbrella and breaking out a glass partition that let her out of the auditorium. She was halfway down the stairs when she said she "heard the roar of the crowd as it came after me. They overtook me, knocked me down, and but for the fact that I was close to the door I think my chance of life would be almost nothing. As it was, I think I walked the last 10 feet to the exit on the bodies of those who had fallen."

It had been John Galvin that railroad Special Agent Peter Quinn had seen running up to a policeman as he passed by the intersection. Because of the many city and county municipal offices, department stores, and nearby theaters, quite a few officers were on foot patrol in the area. Summoned by a chorus of police whistles, officers converged on the theater, arriving there even before the fire department did. Some policemen dashed inside, accompanied by civilian volunteers and reporters, and helped with the early evacuations. Others halted traffic on the street and

The dead on the sidewalk in front of the entrance to the Iroquois Theater. They were being pulled from the wreckage around the doors one at a time

blocked off Randolph Street from two sides. Within hours, there would be hundreds of police officers in and around the theater. Because there were so many female victims, some of Chicago's 30 uniformed police matrons were also called into service.

As the first news of the fire spread through the downtown area and beyond, Randolph Street began to be jammed with horrified crowds of people. They broke through the police lines, trying to see inside. Among them were panicked family members of those who had gone to the

Iroquois that afternoon. As the crowd grew larger, all traffic was halted except for police, fire, and ambulance wagons.

Inside the theater, the badly burned house fireman William Sallers shoved cast and crew members out of the scenery doors and into the alley. By now, he believed that Engine 13 should have arrived, and he stepped outside and began shouting for the commander, Captain Jennings. Sallers believed that if he could get the fire crew through the scenery doors and onto the stage, they could prevent the blaze from reaching the audience. But when he looked behind him, he saw flames roaring out of the doors. He later recalled, "I knew that anybody who was in there was gone. I knew there was no chance to get out."

In the time that had been lost because the Iroquois had no alarm system -- before Engine 13 and other units began arriving -- the theater had turned into an oven. When collecting valuables after the fire, the police found at least a dozen watches that had been stopped at about the same time, 3:50 p.m. This meant that nearly 20 minutes had elapsed from the time that the first alarm had been raised. That certainly accounted for the jamming at the exits and the relatively few people that eyewitnesses saw leaving the theater. Some of the witnesses later stated that nearly seven minutes passed from when they saw fire coming from the roof of the theater and the front doors on Randolph Street being opened.

In those precious minutes, hundreds had died.

7. "DEATH ALLEY"

The gallery and upper balcony of the Iroquois became deathtraps during the fire. They sustained the most significant loss of life because locked doors and gates trapped the patrons who had been seated there. Firefighters later found as many as 200 bodies stacked at the top of the stairs - those who had been unable to escape.

Those who did make it to the fire escape door behind the balcony got a terrifying surprise. The iron ladder that was supposed to be there was missing. The theater had been open

Views from opposite ends of Couch Place during the fire. So many would die in that narrow passage that reporters would soon start calling it "Death Alley"

for nearly six weeks, but no one had bothered to complete the work.

Waiting outside the door was a metal platform, over the edge of which was a sheer drop of 50 feet into Couch Place, the cobblestone alley below.

The narrow alley separated the Iroquois from the Northwestern University building, and the shocked students there had a spectacular view of the horror that was happening next door. There were still a group of students in the building, even though it was the Christmas holiday, along

An illustration of the makeshift ladder bridge that was placed between the buildings by university students and workmen

with a group of painters and workmen repairing damage to some classrooms from an earlier fire.

One of the Northwestern students was George Dunlap, who later recalled, "I was passing one of the classrooms where the painters were, and I looked and saw fire coming out of the theater exits and people fighting to get out, but they were so jammed in, nobody was getting out. I called the painters to let us put some of their planks or ladders across to the fire escapes."

One of the painters seized on George's idea and began calling the other workers for help. He and another man built a makeshift bridge by shoving a 26-foot ladder across the alley to rest on the railing of the fire escape platform.

They watched in horror as a man, "crazed with fear, started to cross the improvised bridge as flames burst out of the exit beneath him." As he started to edge his way across, the ladder slipped off the university building's icy window ledge, and the man plummeted to his death.

After the ladder was lost, three wide boards were pushed across to the theater, and the painters anchored them with their knees.

The first two girls to attempt the crossing were 16-year-old Hortense Lang and her frightened 11-year-old sister, Irene, who she pulled along by the arm. The girls crawled across the planks, shaking with fear. "I was going to jump," Hortense later sobbed, "but I thought of my mother. I just grabbed Irene by the hand and waited for the planks. I don't know how we crossed."

The girls and their mother, who had also escaped the theater, were later reunited in the Northwestern building, where they held hands and wept together for nearly an hour.

The plank bridge worked for a time, but it could not handle the crush of people spilling out of the theater exit. "We went over and tore people loose," said student George Dunlap, "and the painters helped them across the planks. They managed to get 36 people out and laid them on the floor in the classrooms. Some of the women's clothing had been torn away or was burning.

Not knowing what else to do, the students found tubes of Kilfyre that were hanging on hooks and began dumping the powder on the burning victims.

George soon found himself with an unexpected problem. Before blankets and sheets began to arrive from nearby department stores, he recalled that "there were many female victims lying on the floor, naked. Some guy kept gawking at them. I told him three times to get some cans of Kilfyre hanging in the hall. He didn't go. I got mad and swung a half-empty can and it struck him on the forehead and down he went. I figured I had killed him - he laid there for a long time." When the police arrived, George explained what had happened, and one officer was so outraged that he went for his revolver, planning to shoot the unconscious man. Dunlap stopped him by saying that the man was already dead. The officers left, and the man who had been knocked out later woke up and disappeared.

The painters and students helped as many people as they could, but when what sounded like a bomb went off in the theater -- it was the sound of the rigging and scenery falling to the stage -- they watched helplessly as the people trapped inside tried in vain to escape.

What they saw from the windows was something from their worst nightmares.

Those who swarmed from the fire escape exit were pushed to the edge of the railings with nowhere to go. They couldn't turn back because of the crowd behind them, and they were pushed over the side. Some trapped men, women, and children tried to crawl across the planks, but most slipped and fell to the alley below in the confusion and smoke. Others, with their clothing on fire, simply gave up and jumped from the railings.

The boards began falling away, and as the fire grew, flames shot out the doors and out of the windows along the theater's wall. Many of those hoping for rescue were burned alive in full view of the painters and the students. From some of Northwestern University's windows, onlookers could see directly into the theater, which was a solid mass of flames. In the middle of the inferno, they could see men, women, and children running about, and students later said they did not even look human. One of them even described the shapes he could see as "crawling things."

Mrs. F.R. Baldwin of Minneapolis and her mother, both of whom had been seated next to one of the unfinished fire escapes, had only managed to take three or four steps before the crowd behind them pushed them through the exit door. Somehow, neither of the women were seriously hurt. However, Mrs. Baldwin later recalled seeing "a girl lying on one of the fire escape platforms with flames shooting over her through a window." She also saw something else that she would never forget. "One man, who had jumped from a platform that was only six feet from the ground, had not taken two steps before a woman who jumped a moment later from a height of about 40 feet came right down on him, killing him on the spot."

Couch Place was described in one account as a "smoking, flaming hell...too narrow for effective aerial ladder work."

In that alley, swarming with people and littered with the bodies of those who fell to their deaths, theater fireman William Sallers finally found Captain Jennings. Sallers told him that people were cut off and helped Engine 13's pipe men drag the nozzle end of the hose line up the lower metal stairs. The hose was then turned on the people in the alleyway so that the burning clothing could be drenched with water.

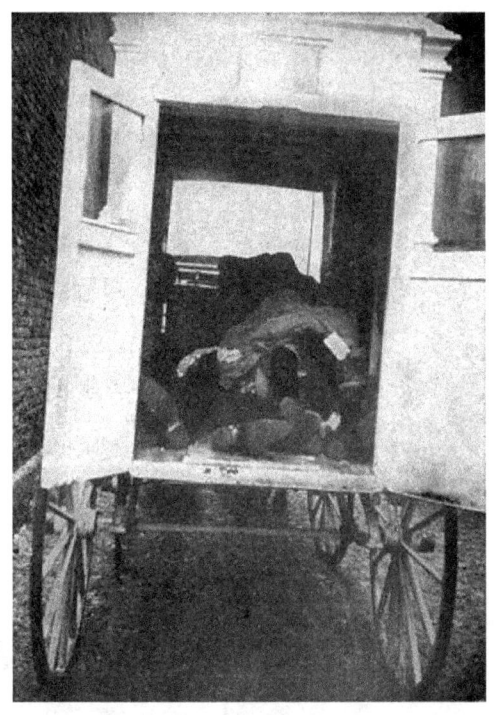

An ambulance loaded with victims that had been picked up in "Death Alley"

Sallers later recounted what happened next: "We heard pounding from behind the iron-shuttered doors and windows. They tried to wrench them open with axes and claw bars. Above them, people, many of whom were being burned alive, were pushed into the unfinished fire escape platform which led nowhere, body after body thudded onto the cobblestones."

The firefighters initially tried to use nets to catch those who fell or jumped, but the nets were made from a black mesh material, and, in the dense smoke, no one could see them. Countless people jumped from the fire escapes that afternoon, and the ones who survived only did so because they landed on the bodies that were starting to pile up on the bricks below.

Crowds gathered to watch the firefighters at work outside of the burning theater

There are no exact figures as to how many made it across the rudimentary bridge from the theater to the university building, but 125 victims were removed from Couch Place that afternoon.

Reporters would later call it "Death Alley."

While firefighters were working to rescue those who tried to flee the theater using the fire escapes, hundreds were still hoping to survive inside the theater.

Ruthie Thompson had no memory of being carried out through the scenery doors, but she did have nightmarish recollections from that day, "Waves of black cloth streamed over me. For one moment, I thought I was dead. But I wasn't even hurt." Ruthie had fallen to the ground and crawled beneath the raised edge of the theater's carriage step. For what must have seemed like hours, the young girl remained wedged into the small opening while "a torrent of people had swept over me. I crouched there until no one else came out and then I stood up and looked around." She described the scene around her as "panic-stricken people, firemen, hoses, swarms of humanity, running up and down the alley."

Inside the theater, one survivor remembered, "the desperate crowd was screaming and pulling off their burnt clothing." She said the stronger ones managed "by strength and endeavor to edge their way our around the jams at the doors - which opened inward." The victims "were piled in a pyramid and others were falling on them. It was an awful sight."

Those "stronger ones" were mostly men. One audience member, D.A. Russell, the Pittsburgh manager of the National Life Insurance Company, stated, "Not a man, as far as I could see, made any effort to save anyone but himself." That was an overstatement, of course, since there is a clear record of many men who helped women and children out of the theater that day at considerable risk to their own lives - but based on how many men trampled everyone in their path on the way to the exit, I can understand his disgust.

Frank Houseman, the former baseball player, turned saloon owner, was one of the brave ones. He had started for an exit on the east side of the building when the fire broke out, but he ran into trouble right away. He told an usher to open the door, but the usher replied, "Wait until the curtain comes down." By this time, the crowd was starting to panic and push against the doors. The stage was burning, and smoke was rolling out into the auditorium.

"For God's sake, open the doors!" Frank shouted at him.

But the usher didn't move. Frank said, "I grabbed the fellow and threw him as far as I could and burst open the door. All I thought of was opening that door, because people at the time were crowding close to me and screaming. I don't remember just how I got that door open, but anyway it opened and carried the crowd out. I felt the latch and found it was like the one on my icebox at home. 'This is easy!' I said to Dexter, who had broken open another door."

Frank and his pal, fellow baseball player Charlie Dexter, stayed by the doors and tried to sort people out so they could get through. As Frank explained, "I tried to do what I could around there for the people being trampled on, trying to pull them apart, and start them on their way if they were not too badly hurt, until others began jumping from the fire escapes above. I could not do very much of anything except to pull out the people being trampled and put them to one side."

Frank remembered one other thing - He and Charlie had been sharing a box with a man and a young woman. He had told the man, "'You'd better bring out the lady.' But the man answered, 'I guess I know my business...' and they stayed behind. God help those two."

Charlie Dexter's harrowing story was similar to his friend's. By the time he had gotten downstairs from the box, he saw Eddie Foy trying to keep the crowd calm from the edge of the stage. "People were running around," Charlie said, "I didn't know what to do, and I ran into a crowd of little children. I saw some draperies, and I opened them. I didn't know where I was going, and I found myself up against some iron doors."

They were some of the side exit doors that the theater's management had "hidden" behind the drapes because they were unattractive. They were also fitted with lock mechanisms that were so complicated even the Iroquois staff members who were supposed to know how to work them were baffled by their complexity.

"I didn't know how to work them," Charlie continued. "The only thing I could see was a crossbar and I started to beat at it. By that time, people were pushed up against me,

IN THE ALLEY OF DEATH AND MUTILATION.
JUMPING FROM THE FIRE ESCAPES TO ESCAPE THE FLAMES.

A news illustration of people fleeing out of the completed fire escapes and into the chaos of "Death Alley"

and I didn't know whether I would be able to get it open or not. I had all the poor little kids around me, and I beat at it until it finally went up, and as it did the people behind me - we went out into the alley. I turned back and saw a wave of fire sweeping over the whole inside of the theater."

Charlie thought he saw Eddie Foy overtaken by the flames in the seconds before the crowd pushed him outside. Luckily, he was wrong about that.

Harriet Bray, the young girl who had come from Indiana to see the show with her father that day, considered herself lucky to get out. When the fire began, her father grabbed her hand, and, with help from a stranger, the three of them made their way through the heat and smoke to one of the fire escapes.

Harriet would always remember the rush of bodies, people pushing, shoving, and knocking others to the floor, and the terror she felt when her father discovered that the fire exit door on their level was jammed. "My father and this other fellow pounded and banged until the door opened," she said. "From there we descended the fire escape only to find that the last flight of steps was also jammed."

With her hair scorched and her dress smoldering, Harriet stood back as her father jumped the last 12 feet to the alley below and then raised his arms to catch her. She was safe a few moments later. She added, "By then, the firemen were on the scene. I'll always remember crawling beneath the legs of the horses who pulled the fire equipment and how they stood motionless in the face of all that chaos."

8. A WALK THROUGH HELL

Captain Edward Buckley of Engine 32 was later credited as the first officer to help with the evacuation of the theater. He never forgot an incident that occurred while this was happening.

Just inside the Randolph Street entrance, one of his men bent down to a woman to hear her last words. "My child," she groaned, "my poor little boy. Is he safe? Tell me he is safe, and I can die."

"He is safe," the fireman replied, choking back tears. The woman died, and he covered her body with a blanket and gently carried her away.

He had no idea what had happened to her son.

Finding their aerial ladders useless, the fire companies that arrived on the scene began dragging their hoses into the front entrance, through the elegant lobby, and up the staircases, trying to get to the burning auditorium. As they tried valiantly to quench the flames, firefighters, police officers, newspaper reporters, and volunteers off the street rescued the survivors - and carried out the dead.

One passerby, Arthur McWilliams, later recounted seeing "people, mostly children, running out of the theater, some with their clothes on fire. Frightened, flaming people ran down the street like wild animals. I was in the middle of the first rope line to enter the theater to try to rescue those inside. We held a rope and each other's hands as we groped into the dense smoke. The first fireman in the line encountered the first little bodies and shouted back; 'There must be a dozen dead in here!' He came out carrying two little scorched bodies, one on each shoulder."

It goes without saying that the first fireman in the line had far under-counted the number of the dead. What McWilliams and the others discovered inside was terrifying.

As the men groped their way up the grand staircase toward the auditorium, they found the smoke so thick that the light from the lanterns they had could barely penetrate it. But what they could see was horrific - glimpses of piles of bodies in doorways, burned skin, smoldering clothing, and blackened faces. Firefighters tugged hose lines up and over the bodies, in some places stacked within two feet of the door frames. From some of the tangled piles of scorched people, they could hear moans. The stench of roasted flesh was everywhere, missed with the industrial smells of charred hemp, cloth, and paint.

Contemporary illustration of a Chicago firefighter carrying out the dead from the theater

The firemen, police officers, and volunteers picked their way carefully through the theater. They stayed close to the floor to avoid the smoke and pressed handkerchiefs to their noses and mouths. When corridors converged, they found bodies stacked to 10 feet deep. There were victims everywhere, some horribly disfigured, and many whose clothing had been torn off them in the mad rush to escape.

Many men wept openly as they searched for life, and others were so unnerved that they fled from the building.

And is it any wonder?

Death had claimed hundreds in a matter of minutes. Some of those trapped in the theater died from inhaling smoke or fumes from burning scenery and chemicals. Others were trampled or trapped beneath a pile of bodies in a doorway. Scores of them burned to death. For them, at least, the end had come quickly.

But all of those among the dead would haunt the dreams of the living who entered the theater that afternoon for many years to come.

Bishop Samuel Fallows from St. Paul's Reformed Episcopal Church was one of the volunteers that went into the building that afternoon. He had been passing by the theater when the call went out for volunteers, and he pitched in, not realizing the extent of the damage inside until he entered the auditorium.

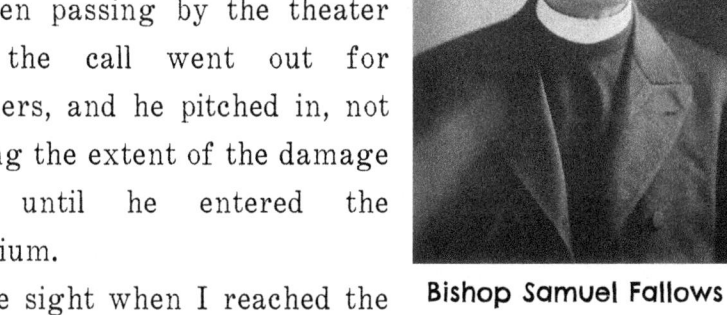

Bishop Samuel Fallows

"The sight when I reached the balconies was pitiful beyond description," he later told a reporter for the *Tribune*. "It grew in horror as I looked over the seats. The bodies were in piles. Women had their hands over their faces as if to shield off a blow. Children lay crushed beneath their parents, as if they had been hurled to the marble floors."

As he surveyed the auditorium, he was overwhelmed by memories from the past. He explained, "I saw the great battlefields of the Civil War, but they were nothing to this. When we began to take out the bodies, we found that many of the audience had been unable to get even near the exits. Women were bent over the seats, their fingers clenched on the iron sides so strongly that they were torn and bleeding. Their faces and clothes were burned, and they must have suffered intensely."

A volunteer named William Corbett would later describe how he had been there to help carry out the victims and had tried to dislodge the body of a young boy from one of the piles of the dead. The child's skin simply peeled off in his hands.

A husband and wife had died so tightly locked in one another's arms that their bodies had to be carried out together.

A woman had thrown her arms around her child in a vain effort to save her. Both had been burned beyond recognition.

The sight of all the children's bodies broke down the composure of the most veteran of the rescuers. Tears ran down the faces of police officers, firefighters, and bystanders as tiny body after tiny body was carried out of the Iroquois. Their small hands were often clenched at their

The devastated auditorium after the fire

face in what had been a fruitless attempt to ward off the heat from the blaze.

Some of the men begged to give up. The fathers among them were too shattered by the deaths of so many children. Others claimed that the bodies of the dead could not be untangled.

Chief O'Neill and Police Captain Herman Schuettler took charge of the situation and ordered the men to get the dead out of the way so that the living might somehow be found. It had to be done, he said. He told two of his men to grab hold of a dead man and pull him out. Two burly firemen seized the body by the shoulders and struggled and pulled until the corpse was free. Then they moved another body -

and another and another. A terrible moan was heard from somewhere in the pile.

"For God's sake," Chief O'Neill cried out, "Get down to that one who's alive!"

Police officers pulled off their heavy overcoats and worked frantically, pulling arms and legs and hauling bodies from the heap. As fast as they were freed, one policeman - or sometimes two or three - would stagger down the stairs with the corpses.

Legendary Chicago firefighter Chief Francis O'Neill

Then, from out of the pile of bodies came a fireman with something in his arms. "Out of the way, men! Let me out," he called. "This kid's alive!"

The workers fell back, and the fireman crawled over the heap and was helped out. He ran down the steps two at a time to get the child to a place where they could be helped before it was too late. Other firefighters from inside the theater passed out more bodies, which were handed from one policeman to another until some on the outside of the heap could take the dead and carry them downstairs.

A policeman who had been pulling at the heap of bodies shouted, "I've got her, chief! She's alive, all right!"

"Easy there, men, easy," cried Captain Schuettler," but hurry and get that woman to a doctor."

The young woman they had all heard moaning in the pile was around 18 years old, and she was crying softly as she was pulled clear of the bodies. A fireman scooped her up and, holding her tightly in his arms, hurried her outside to a medical station.

"There must be more alive!" O'Neill urged the men. "Work hard, boys!"

The men hardly had to be told. Urged on by the discovery of two people still alive, they began pulling and hauling as if their own lives depended on it.

Reporters - the only ones in the theater besides the volunteers, police officers, and firefighters - put away their pencils and notebooks and pitched in, carrying the dead down the wet, slippery stairs to the outside. Newspaper artists tossed away their sketchbooks to jump in and pick up the feet or head of a body that was too heavy for one of the firefighters to carry alone. The stream of men constantly flowed up and down the stairs. Usually, two men supported a body, but one of the larger men often was seen with bodies clung over their shoulders.

"Isn't that girl alive?" Chief O'Neill asked one man.

"No, she's dead," a fireman replied quietly as he carried her toward the staircase. "Poor thing. God rest her soul."

But halfway down the steps, two arms suddenly clasped the fireman's neck. He was so startled that he almost fell.

After the fire – a view of the stage from the burned-out balcony of the Iroquois. An inspection tour of the theater was taken by fire and city officials after the tragedy

He likely would have if a nearby police officer hadn't steadied him.

"She's alive! She's alive!" the firefighter shouted. "Get out of the way, there, out of the way, men!" He dashed out of the front doors and took the girl to the closest aid station at a nearby drug store.

From the moment the two men had entered the auditorium, Chief O'Neill and Fire Marshal Musham had been calling out orders. O'Neill demanded more lanterns, doctors,

Every kind of wagon that could be found was used to carry away the injured – and the dead. They were taken to nearby stores, saloons, restaurants, which were turned into temporary hospitals and morgues

nurses, blankets, and police wagons. Musham called for additional men and fire equipment and for every available ambulance, wagon, and delivery truck to be sent to the theater. By now, there were as many as 12 fire engines and five hook and ladder trucks at the scene.

As the requests for assistance spread, the public's response was immediate and overwhelming. A nearby medical school sent 100 students to help the doctors who had been dispatched to the Iroquois. A hardware company down the street emptied its stock of 200 lanterns. Marshall Field's, Mandel Brothers, Carson, Pirie, Scott, and other department stores sent blankets, sheets, rolls of linen, packages of cotton, and large delivery wagons. They converted their ground-floor restrooms and lounges into emergency medical stations. Nearby hotels and businesses did the same. Montgomery Ward sent one of its new, motorized delivery wagons to the scene, but even with its bell ringing, it could not get through the crowds that were jammed into the streets and had to turn back. Other bodies were taken away by police wagons and ambulances and transported to a temporary morgue at Marshall Field's on State Street.

Within a short time, restaurants, saloons, and stores in the vicinity of the Iroquois had been turned into improvised aid stations as medical workers and volunteers began arriving in large numbers. Chicago's central telephone exchange was overwhelmed by emergency calls - and by those spreading the news of the horror that had occurred at the Iroquois.

Author and poet Edgar Lee Masters was a practicing attorney in Chicago at the time and later remembered, "The estimate of those who lost their lives started at a small number. But every few minutes added to the list. When it reached 60 the people in the street and city were horror-stricken, but then it began to mount into the hundreds and beyond."

In the toy department at Marshall Field's, the little girl from Galesburg, Dorsha Hayes, whose mother had refused to let her family attend the show at the Iroquois, was too young to understand what was happening. Her parents started to realize that something was wrong when the salesclerks began whispering among themselves and leaving their counters to look out the store's windows to the street. As the news spread from department to department, Mr. and Mrs. Hayes finally learned what a close call they'd had. Years later, Dorsha would say that her mother never could explain her premonition that day.

Even though an entire stock of lanterns had been donated to the recovery effort at the theater, they were not bright enough to cut through the smoke and gloom. After some calls were made, the Edison company rushed over a batch of 40 arc lamps and, when they were turned on, fire and rescue workers were stunned by what they saw. Deputy Fire Marshal John Campion looked around and then crossed himself. "Oh, dear Jesus," he muttered, "have mercy on their souls."

Dead audience members were sitting in their seats, facing the stage, their eyes staring blankly ahead. Others had no burn marks on them -- they had suffocated from the smoke. Many women were found with their heads resting on the back of the seat in front of them. One woman was bent back over the seat she had been sitting in, her spine severed. A young boy's head was missing. Hundreds had been trampled. One face bore the imprint of a shoe heel, and other faces had been so battered they were unrecognizable. Many more had been burned beyond recognition.

Police officers sorting out the jewelry, cash, and valuables left behind by the dead. While most items were traced to their owners, some of it ended up in the pockets of unscrupulous and ghoulish "volunteers"

Clothing, shoes, pocketbooks, and other personal belongings were strewn about. After the fire was completely out, at least six bushel-sized baskets of items were found in the theater and collected by the police. One officer recalled seeing two large barrels of shoes. For days, officials sifted through the charred remains of the auditorium, looking for rings, necklaces, lockets, and coins. They used gold pans and sieves, the same methods employed in the gold fields out west. There were ten baskets of money and jewelry that were picked up from the main floor.

The belongings that did remain in the pockets of the dead made them targets for thieves. In the confusion, some of the men who entered the theater as "volunteers" were there for another agenda - robbing the dead. The press dubbed them "ghouls," and most were chased away by the firefighters or were arrested on the spot for pocketing money and jewelry and even for trying to pry the rings from victim's fingers.

Sadly, not all the thieves were civilians from the street. George Dunlap, the college student who had helped set up the plank bridge between the university building and the unfinished fire door platform, would never forget what he saw happen that afternoon. "I worked all day and all night carrying out bodies," he later said. "I still can't get over seeing some policemen taking money out of women's pocketbooks and throwing the pocketbooks away."

George may have been shocked by what he saw but based on the amount of corruption in the Chicago Police Department in those days - I'm not.

The men working in the auditorium never forgot what they saw either.

Many of the victims' hands were clenched and outstretched as if trying to protect themselves from the fire. All the fabric on one of the couches in a passageway had been burned away, except for one spot where two dead children were found with the kneeling body of their mother, who had desperately tried to shield them from the flames.

At the edge of the auditorium, a fireman emerged from the ashes with the body of a little girl in his arms. He groped his way forward, stumbling toward Fire Marshall William Henry Musham, who ordered him to give the child to someone else and get back to work. The fireman, in some kind of daze, kept walking. Another senior officer also ordered him to hand the child off to someone else. But when the fireman came closer, Musham and the other officers could see the streaks of tears on the man's soot-covered face. "I'm sorry, chief," the man said, "but I've got a little one like this at home. I want to carry this one out."

Musham told him to go ahead, and the men stepped aside. The weeping fireman carried the little body down the steps of what only an hour before had been the glittering promenade of the grandest theater in Chicago.

With help from the Edison lights, Deputy Marshal Campion walked through the theater's still-smoking auditorium while his men continued to douse hot spots that occasionally burst into flame.

"Is there any living person here?" Campion shouted.

There was no reply.

"If anyone here is alive," he called out again, "groan or make some sound and we'll take you out."

He looked around the auditorium, taking in the burned seats, the blackened walls, the twisted piles of debris on the stage, and the smoldering bodies of the dead.

But the devastated Iroquois Theater was silent.

It had taken just 15 minutes for the fire to end the lives of 572 people. More of those who attended the show that afternoon died later, bringing the death toll up to 602. The dead numbered more than those who had perished in the Great Fire of 1871.

And there were 212 children among the dead.

In addition, hundreds more had been injured in what was supposed to be a "fireproof" theater - perhaps the safest in the city.

Earlier on that cold winter morning, the Iroquois had been a "temple of beauty" and a "palace of the arts," but as the Associated Press would report later that evening, it now looked like "a burned-out volcano crater."

9. ALL THE NEWS THAT'S FIT TO PRINT

Charles Collins, a recently hired general assignment reporter for the *Chicago Record-Herald,* found himself entrenched in the story of the Iroquois Theater fire. He had been at the theater on opening night, and the young reporter - who had just turned 20-years-old - had been amazed by not only the city's notables in attendance but with the theater itself. He had, quite honestly, never seen anything like it before.

It was a feeling that would be repeated for him on the afternoon of December 30, 1903. He had never seen anything like what he saw outside the Iroquois that day --- and likely never would again.

An hour earlier, he had been at the theater, talking to one of the owners about ticket scalping, but now he found himself in a wet, muddy Randolph Street that was choked by wagons, fire engines, and crowds of people who watched in shock as one blanket-covered corpse after another was carried out of the building's main entrance.

He later wrote, "The bodies extended about 100 yards on either side of the theater's entrance. A long line of horse-drawn vehicles waiting to haul the dead or dying to hospitals, morgues, and funeral parlors." He estimated that the crowd standing in Randolph Street numbered as many as 5,000 people.

"They were gazing at the theater," he noted, "absolutely quiet, hushed as if they were in awe. There was total silence."

A few men, but mostly women and children, often with most of their clothing missing or badly injured, were taken next door to Thompson's Restaurant, which, in just 15 minutes, had been converted from an eatery to a first aid receiving station.

When Collins heard what had happened at the theater, he first called his editor to confirm the rumors were true. The editor, Al Bergener, told him that yes, there had been an alarm, and there seemed to be trouble. He told Collins to come into the office, and by the time he arrived there - he'd only been four blocks away - Bergener was frantic. He ordered Collins to get to the theater and "to find survivors." He went directly to Thompson's.

The scene inside of the restaurant was both unimaginable and horrific. Men, women, and children were lying along the walls and splayed out on tabletops as doctors, nurses, and medical students cared for the injured and cleared away the dead to make room for those who were continuing to be brought in from the theater next door. The shouts of the doctors were only drowned out by the shrieks of pain. Clothing was cut away, and burns were treated with olive oil and then wrapped in cotton. Small quantities of brandy and other aids were used to revive those who were unconscious but still breathing. Nurses and students held small mirrors under the victims' nostrils to check for signs of life. If the wounded failed to fog up the glass, the body was wrapped in a blanket and moved aside to make room for the next person.

One eyewitness to the morbid scene later recounted, "Some were charred beyond recognition, some only scorched, and others black from suffocation; some crushed in the rush of panic, others... the broken remains of those who leaped to death. And most of them were in the forms of women and children. So fast came the bodies for a time that there was one steady stream of persons carried in. There was the figure of a man with broad shoulders and dressed in black whose entire face was burned away, only the back of his head remaining to show he ever had a head; yet below the shoulders he was untouched by the fire. There lay women with their arms gone, or their legs, while one had side burned off, with only the cross-shoulder bone remaining. She had worn a pink silk waist and black skirt; the fragments of the garment still clung to her like a shroud. There was a little boy, with a shock of red-brown hair, whose tiny mouth was open in terror and whose baby hands were burned off so that his tiny wrists showed like red stumps."

Such descriptions are enough to give anyone nightmares - imagine what it was like to see these things first-hand.

Charles Collins went into the restaurant's kitchen where one of the cooks was calmly peeling potatoes in a corner, presumably for that night's dinner service. A weeping father was there being treated for burns. Charles wrote the man's name down on a small piece of paper he'd found - he'd rushed out of the office without his notebook - and tried to reassure the man that the daughter he'd been separated from when they fled the Iroquois was probably safe.

Amazingly, a few minutes later, when Charles was venturing into the depth of "Death Alley," he passed by a paint shop that had been turned into a first-aid station. Through the window, he saw a "very bright and intelligent girl of seven or eight who was walking around with a little olive oil on the bridge of her nose, which was slightly scorched." For some reason, the young reporter went inside to talk to her and learned that the girl had lost her father in the flight from the theater. On a hunch, he asked a nurse if he could take the child across the alley to the restaurant.

The distraught father that Charles had just met was the father of the little girl. He left them to tearfully reunite, and he never saw them again.

Meanwhile, stories of tragedy and heroism were still playing out inside and outside of the theater.

In Thompson's Restaurant, the Ohio Wesleyan student from Buenos Aires, William McLaughlin, was dying. A young medical student who was caring for him noticed the Delta Tau Delta fraternity pin on his lapel and said, "I'd better take off your frat pin, old man. Someone might take it if you go, you know."

"No, I guess not," William replied. "It's been a friend of mine for quite a while, and I'd not like to have it taken off now. Just let it stay on to the finish."

He was still wearing the pin when he died.

Dr. E.E. Vaughn was working inside the restaurant, doing all he could for those suffering and making room for the living by moving the dead. He had just carried the body of a child to a place along the far wall of the room when he spotted something he hadn't expected to see. "Men, there's a live one in there!" he shouted, and while others came running, Dr. Vaughn began to pull aside bodies until he uncovered a woman of middle age, terribly burned around the face and her clothing a mass of charred shreds.

The woman was quickly carried over to a table, and oxygen began to be pumped into her lungs. Two doctors worked her arms like pumps while a nurse manipulated her heart. She finally started to breathe on her own, and her heartbeat became stronger. After a minute, her eyelids began to move, and a groan escaped her lips.

"She lives!" said Dr. Vaughn and ordered brandy to be forced into her throat. She had been saved from death but would suffer terribly from her burns.

She managed to say that her name was Harbaugh before she was taken away to a hospital.

Like Episcopal Bishop Samuel Fallows, the Reverend J.P. Muldoon, Auxiliary Bishop of Chicago, was another church officials on hand when the fire occurred. Bishop Muldoon was also passing by the theater and, without hesitating, rushed inside, climbed over corpses, and entered the smoke-filled auditorium to administer the last rites to the dying while the firefighters were still extinguishing flames. He was asked

Reverend J.P. Muldoon

to leave for his own safety several times, but he refused. Finally, several firefighters bodily carried him outside because they feared that a wall might collapse.

Muldoon was later commended by the Pope for his bravery and selflessness in the face of danger.

Also, like Bishop Fallows, Dr. H.L. Montgomery had served during the Civil War. He was one of the first physicians at the scene of the fire. He compared what he saw to the battlefields of the war and added, "I rescued 150 people during the Chicago fire. I have seen the wreckage of explosions. But I never saw anything so grimly horrible as this."

"When the fire broke out, I was taking tickets at the door," said usher E. Lovett. "The crowd began to move toward exists on the ground floor, and I rushed to the big entrance doors and threw three of them open. From there, I hurried to the cigar store and called up the police and fire departments."

Lovett hurried back to the theater to provide more help, but when he tried to get more of the doors open, he was shoved aside. The crowd was frenzied at that point, and there was nothing to do to hold them in check while he tried to get more doors opened. "Conditions on the balconies must have been appalling. They were well-filled, but the exists, had they been opened, would have proved ample for all."

Lovett managed to help open the doors from the lobby to the street before being nearly crushed by the crowds. He stayed at the scene for as long as he could, unlike many of the other ushers, who fled for their own safety, leaving locked doors behind them.

A man who only offered the name "Chester" was attending the theater that day with his wife and two daughters. They had been sitting in the lower balcony of the auditorium, and in the panic, he managed to get his wife and daughter to the fire escape. But almost as soon as they ran out onto the metal landing, fire swept out from a window below them and set the clothing of his wife and daughters on fire. Burned himself, Chester fought the flames until realizing that if they continued to delay on the fire escape, they would undoubtedly die. He pushed his family down the ladder - only to find that it came to a sudden end about 10 feet from the ground. The fire escape had never been completed.

Chester reached out, grabbed his girls by their hands, and lowered them as far as he could - and let go. Both girls tumbled the final few feet to the alley. He dropped his wife and then jumped himself.

Luckily, W.G. Smith of the Chicago Teaming Company on Dearborn Street saw them jump, and with some of his men, he picked up the family and took them into his store. The fire department was now just starting to arrive.

After ensuring that Chester and his family were safe, Smith hurried back to the Couch Place alley to find that same fire escape was now filled with screaming and struggling women. They were being scorched and burned by the flames rushing from the windows. He shouted to them to wait - the firemen were coming - but one woman jumped as he was shouting. She was also taken to Smith's store. Her injuries were minor.

As Smith was carrying the woman to safety, his assistant, Morris Eckstrom, and the engineer of the university building, M.J. Tierney, ran to help the women on the fire escape. The firemen were still trying to get organized, and the screams of the women were simply too frightful to hear without offering help.

Eckstrom shouted up to the ladies. "Jump one by one and we'll catch you!"

Tierney brought a blanket with him, and the two men stretched it out as best they could. The women, realizing it was their only chance, began to jump. Some of them were injured but, thanks to the two men, none were seriously hurt.

"I know we caught 20 women that way, before the flames got so terrific that none of them could reach the fire escape," Morris Eckstrom later said. "I saw a dozen women and children and some men, through the open door to the fire escape, fall back into the flames."

Charles Collins, the reporter for the *Chicago Record-Herald*, wrote about his experiences at Thompson's Restaurant and in "Death Alley," but he made his final stop of that day at the Sherman House, where Eddie Foy had retreated after the fire broke out. Collins wrote that Eddie was "hysterical" in the wake of the blaze and had suffered superficial burns.

Eddie told Collins and other reporters, "I never saw anything happen so quickly as that fire. It was like a flash in the pan, and the entire theater was in flames, men were screaming, and women were fainting. It reminded me of the Chicago fire."

Eddie wept as he spoke about finding his son in the freezing alley and as they started walking toward the hotel, a kindly passerby offered him his overcoat. Eddie's wife was just leaving the hotel to go to the theater with two of his children when he and Bryan arrived. He remembered getting greasepaint on his wife's face as the two of them tearfully embraced. In a daze at the hotel, he had handed the borrowed overcoat back to the man who had offered it to him, but to the end of his life, he regretted not asking that man his name so that he could send him a personal letter of gratitude.

When Charles returned to the office, his editor told him to get busy writing about "escapes and rescues." The newspaper was overwhelmed with reports, and he was sent to his desk with a large batch of Chicago City Press

Association reports. "I remembered everything I saw," Charles said and began writing about the father-daughter reunion that he helped with before tackling the wire copy. The newsroom was eerily quiet that night. Only the clattering echo of a handful of typewriters could be heard. Charles considered himself fortunate to be working on rewrites with other staff reporters who were out on the depressing, exhausting task of seeking victim identifications at morgues, hospitals, and funeral parlors across the city. He said, "Many reporters worked all that night, all the next day, and the following night" as they pieced together the story and added names to the growing list of victims.

For some reporters, the story became personal. Frank Moore, who worked for the Associated Press, had been called in from his usual beat at the Stockyards to cover the disaster. Later in the evening, he was asked by some friends whose daughter had been at the theater if he could go to the morgue and check to see if she was there.

She probably was, but Frank couldn't tell for sure.

"She was so badly burned I was unable to recognize her," he later admitted. "Her folks never got a positive identification, but they buried her, thinking she might be their daughter."

One exhausted telegraph operator for Western Union worked without stopping throughout the afternoon and evening, sending endless details around the country. He returned home late that night to find that his own wife had been one of the victims of the fire.

A note in the *Chicago InterOcean* summed up the horror: "With tears in their eyes, and with faltering voices, thousands of people thronged the newspaper last night, inquiring for missing relatives and friends, trying to secure one little article of information of missing ones, and hoping against hope they would receive favorable replies. More often than not, the news was bad."

But fortunately, not in every case.

Ruthie Thompson remained hidden under the carriage step in front of the theater for nearly an hour, shivering in the cold but too frightened to come out. She was eventually discovered by a volunteer and was carried to a nearby aid station, where she found her Aunt Abby. Like Ruthie, Abby had made it to safety through the stage exit. Ruthie's little brother, John, had been picked up by a kindly man inside the theater, and he had lifted the boy high in the air and passed him to other adults, hand over hand so that he passed over the heads of the struggling and screaming mob and went right out the theater's front doors. Aunt Dot had escaped through the front lobby. And miraculously, Grandpa Holloway - who hadn't approved of the theater from the start - had walked out the stage entrance and was found waiting patiently in Couch Place, watching Engine 13 pump water into the Iroquois' smoking interior.

Ruthie's father, George, had first learned about the fire from someone on the street as he walked toward his office. Ignoring the heavy traffic and icy streets, he ran out into the middle of State Street, sprinted the length of the block to Randolph, and elbowed his way through the crowd outside the theater, shouting, "Get out of my way! My children are in there!"

His passage was blocked by a half-dozen police officers. A fireman that he recognized stopped him, too, and sadly told George, "No, Mr. Thompson, you can't go in. There's not a soul alive in there now."

Crazed with fear and breathing heavily, George passed the dead and dying and went to the rear of his restaurant next door. He climbed the steps to the bakery and spotted a ladder that had been rigged from one of his windows to the theater. It had helped a few people escape. He suddenly decided that he would use it to get into the theater and find his children.

George climbed onto the ladder on his hands and knees, prepared to start easing his way across when he felt a hand grab hold of him. It was the baker, a heavy-set man who had worked for him for years.

"Let me go!" George shouted at him. "My children are in there!"

"No," the baker said. "No one is alive in there now."

But George wasn't hearing this. "You're fired!" he shouted at the baker.

The other man shrugged but refused to let him go. "Then I'm fired - but you're not going in there."

At that moment, the restaurant manager rushed into the room. He cried out, gasping for air. "All of them got out! They were all in here, and they've gone to your office and are waiting there."

Ruthie later recalled, "When father burst into the office, my two aunts and I fell on him, weeping hysterically. My brother cried, too. The only calm person was my grandfather, who was sitting in a straight-backed office chair. He merely waited until the storm was over."

And then almost undoubtedly told his son-in-law, "I told you so."

On the morning of December 31, those who had not seen the news in the "Extra!" editions on the previous night or had only heard it through word of mouth were stunned by the banner headlines. Chicago, for the first time in its history, prepared to welcome the New Year in silence. There would be no greetings of "Happy New Year" at the start of 1904.

On the front page of the *Chicago Tribune* was a list of the dead, along with the names of 200 people who had been injured, many of whom were not expected to survive. It also offered a box ad that identified 13 places that were holding the remains of victims. The editor noted, "Of the dead, less than 100 were identified last night. Of the unidentified, nearly all were so badly burned that recognition was impossible. Only by trinkets and burned scraps of wearing apparel will the bodies of hundreds be made known to their families. Never has the city received a blow so instantaneously shocking."

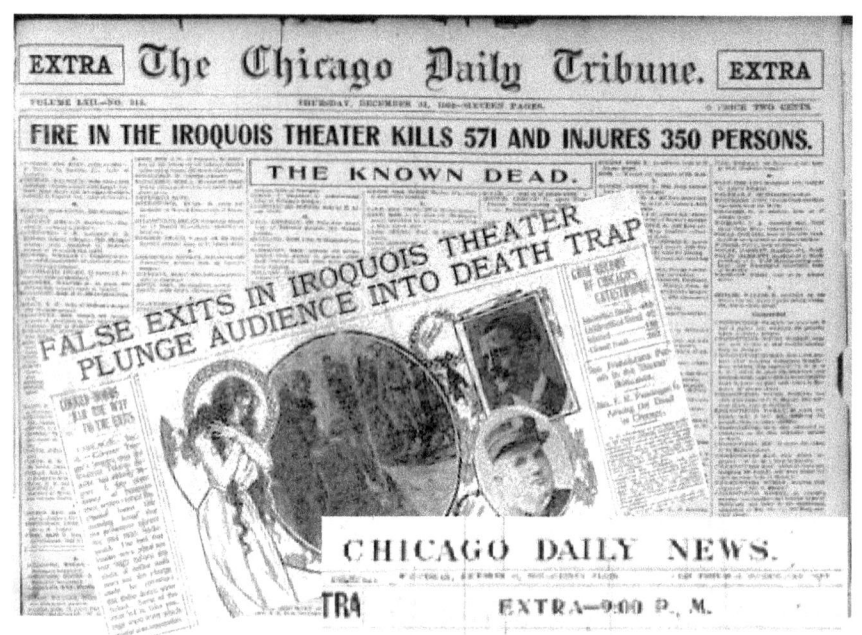

Mayor Harrison hurried home by train from Oklahoma and declared a citywide week of mourning. There would be no unnecessary noise, including band music, the blowing of horns, and train, boat, and factory whistles. Flags were lowered to half-mast. No celebrations were allowed for the

New Year. The Board of Education delayed the start of the new semester out of respect for the 40 teachers and principals who had perished in the fire. Most shops were closed for the week. The only exceptions were stores in the Loop, which were only open to sell funeral accouterments like candles and crepe.

The striking livery and hearse drivers declared a 10-day truce and returned to work, many of them refusing payment for their services. Hearses were offered - white for children and black for adults - from all over the Midwest. Hundreds of carriages were now traveling toward cemeteries all over the Chicago area.

The *Tribune* said, "This frightful thing was over before the city knew it happened. The news left paralysis behind."

In the *New York Clipper*: "Chicago enters upon the New Year silently, dumb with the shock of disaster and speechless with the anguish of sudden and awful calamity - lives sacrificed to someone's carelessness."

Of those who had attended the performance that day, 150 of the dead were men, three times that were women, and worst of all, 150 were children. The horror cut across all class lines. Bankers and wealthy executives searched morgues alongside clerks and domestic servants.

The combined magic of wireless and cable spread the news of the disaster to all parts of the world. Telegrams of condolence flooded in from foreign cities and heads of state, many from nations whose citizens were leaving to begin new lives in the United States. Messages arrived from the King and Queen of England, the Russian Czar, the German Kaiser, the king of Italy, the president of France, and leaders from all the Scandinavian countries. President Theodore Roosevelt telegraphed Mayor Harrison to express the nation's sorrow.

But the people of Chicago were numbed with shock. The outpouring of sympathy was not enough to ease the heartbreak of those who were still searching for family members, friends, and loved ones among the dead.

10. SEARCHING AMONG THE DEAD

The dead were carried away from the ruins of the Iroquois Theater in just about anything with wheels. They were picked up from the sidewalk in front of the theater, the alley behind it, and from Thompson's Restaurant next door. It was quickly realized that police patrol wagons and ambulances were simply not going to be enough, so Chief O'Neill and Coroner John E. Traeger sent men out to stop drays and delivery wagons and press them into service. Transfer companies were asked to send wagons, and the department stores on State Street sent their delivery trucks.

The bodies - outstretched on sidewalks and covered with blankets - were placed in the wagons. As soon as space was made by the removal of one body, two more were there to fill it.

One of the wagons that belonged to the Dixon Transfer Company became so heavily loaded with the dead that the two big horses pulling it could not start it rolling. Police officers and spectators put their shoulders to the wheel.

Once the drays were filled and moving, there was difficulty getting them through the crowds on Randolph Street. Even those inside the fire lines that the police had established. It took police officers with clubs to walk ahead of the wagons and force an opening among the hundreds of men who had sent their wives and children to the theater that day and feared one of the wagons might carry the remains of their own family.

Eight or more wagons at a time were backed up to the curb, waiting for loads of the dead. Two police officers would seize a blanket at the corners and swing it - with its contents - up to two other men who were waiting in the wagon. This would be repeated until a wagonload of bodies had been handled. Then the police forced a way through the crowds as another wagon took its place.

On the nights that followed the fire, the people of Chicago shambled forward in shock. Hundreds of men and women held lonely vigils in frigid weather on the last two nights of the year, waiting to identify lost relatives and friends - all

Anxious relatives and friends waited in line for hours, trying to get into the morgues to look for the missing and dead

laid out in neat rows, covered by blankets. At the rear of one funeral parlor, 182 bodies were placed in four rows deep on the floor.

Panicked and worried relatives swamped the Chicago authorities with telephone calls. Getting little satisfaction, they called the newspapers, but most of their pleas went unanswered. There was simply too much chaos and too many unknowns.

The bodies were scattered to undertakers and morgues throughout the city.

At the morgues, "men showed less hope and courage as a rule than the women did. Mothers rushed breathless down

Bodies of Iroquois Fire victims were placed in long lines. Any items found with the bodies were put on display to make identification of the often badly burned bodies easier

(Below Left) The police were overwhelmed with the number of victims and worked hard to keep track of them

long rows of victims searching for children, but fathers, sons, and brothers often turned from the doors, lacking the courage to go in. In some morgues lay whole families, and in other cases, a father or mother sat alone at home with the remainder of the family dead."

Many arranged for their doctors or dentists to accompany them to make identifications of the dead. Many who made the trip to private funeral parlors in the evening were turned away and told to "come back in the morning."

At that point, the casualty figures were difficult, if not impossible, to determine. An unknown audience member who might have been counted among the dead, injured or missing could have been removed from the scene by a family member. Or they could have managed to get home on their own. Or could have wandered around the Loop for ours in a daze before they were discovered.

Adding to the difficulties of making an accurate count, the victims' bodies had been taken to so many different places in the city - shops, restaurants, businesses, and even department stores. They were taken to a dozen morgues and likely more than twice that many funeral parlors.

This left the families - the grieving fathers, mothers, aunts, uncles, and children - to travel wherever they could as they searched for their beloved dead.

By late evening on December 30, 135 bodies were lying on the floors of Jordan's Funeral Home on East Madison Street. The first were brought in ambulances and police patrol wagons. Later, they came in delivery wagons and two-horse trucks, and it quickly became evident that the place would soon be filled to capacity. Across the alley, police officers found an open saloon, kicked out the customers, and pressed it into service as a temporary morgue.

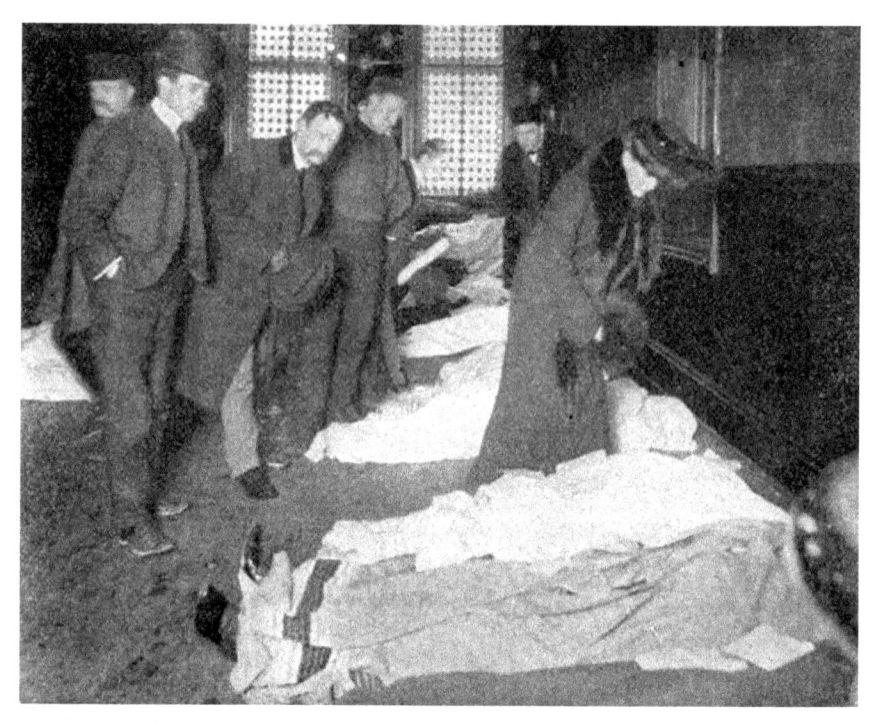

A grieving mother at Jordan's Funeral Home looks at the faces of dozens of children, hoping to find her own

Two policemen oversaw each load of the dead, and as soon as the first bodies were received, they began searching for identification. Jewelry and valuables, as well as letters, cards, and other papers, were put into sealed envelopes and marked with a number that corresponded to a tag attached to the body. When this work was completed, the envelopes were sent to police headquarters. Those who came to inquire about missing relatives and friends were sent to City Hall to inspect the envelopes.

The scene at Jordan's, the annex across the alley, and at undertaking establishments across the city were strikingly similar - and always tragic. Many of the bodies from the theater were badly burned and disfigured, almost all the faces were discolored, and the clothing was torn, rumpled, and wet. Nearly all of them were women and children. The men were few. In many cases, their hands were torn, as if violent efforts had been made to cling savagely to life.

As quickly as the work of searching the bodies was completed, the attendants stretched strips of cloth over the still and silent forms, partially hiding what writers called "the pitiful horror of the sight."

Reporters assigned to cover the morgues wrote that while there were occasional outbursts of grief and hysteria after the body of a relative or friend was found, most people silently filed past the rows of the dead, searching for familiar faces, articles of clothing, or personal items.

As the crowds increased, many began to be turned away. It would have been impossible for all who came to inspect the bodies at once because they were so close together. Women unable to get inside wept and beat on the front window glass of the undertaking parlors, only to be turned away and told to come back later.

At Jordan's, two women fainted in chairs in an outer office. They had come looking for family members but had been overwhelmed by the long lines of the dead.

The telephone bell ran incessantly with calls from people whose relatives had failed to return home on time. They begged for news, describing faces, clothing, and jewelry.

George E. McMauglan was an attorney for the Chicago and Rock Island Railroad and was one of the first parents to arrive at Jordan's Funeral Home. He was looking for his daughter, Helen. A friend who had been near the theater when the fire started later discovered Helen's body at Thompson's Restaurant. He attached a card with her name on it to her body, left her in the care of one of the doctors, and went to telephone McMauglan. But when he returned, the body was gone, and the two men spent the entire night trying to find the young woman's remains.

They never did.

At Rolston's undertaking rooms on Adams Street, 182 bodies had been laid out in three and four rows deep. Men, women, and children were tagged with numbers and waited for identification. Over the lines of the dead, the police hovered, searching for names and valuables. Most of the bodies were only partly covered by blankets.

A huge crowd surged outside that first evening, struggling with the police and demanding to be allowed to enter. When Coroner Traeger arrived, he began to allow groups of 12 to 15 people inside at one time.

The task of identifying the dead who were removed from the Iroquois went on for days. Family members had no idea where all of the bodies were taken and had to go from place to place, searching for any sign of their loved ones.

In the undertaking rooms of J.C. Gavin and the Carroll Brothers, on North Clark and Wells Street, 54 bodies had been sent to await identification. By midnight on December 30, only nine of them had been recognized by the hundreds of friends and relatives who filed through the rooms.

At Sheldon's undertaking parlor on West Madison Street, 47 bodies - some of them with their clothing completely burned away and most with features charred beyond recognition - were placed on display for grieving loved ones. Only five of the bodies were men. The rest of them were all women and children.

By late that night, only four had been identified.

There were similar scenes taking place at all the undertaking rooms where the bodies had been taken. An atmosphere of despair seemed to permeate these places.

The stories of the dead - and of the living - were heartbreaking.

Hours after the fire, a man who had been pronounced dead at Thompson's suddenly "returned to life" and found himself wrapped in a blanket in the back of a wagon hauling bodies to a funeral parlor. He pushed two corpses off his chest and cried out for "air!"

The startled driver immediately had him removed from the wagon and sent to a nearby hospital by ambulance.

Chicago schoolteacher Rita Wild successfully escaped from the Iroquois and went home on her own with what were described as "minor burns." She was examined by her family doctor, who assured her she would recover.

Rita died from shock four days later.

Two frightened young girls from Aurora, Illinois, ages 12 and 14, walked into a manufacturing company near the theater on the day of the fire. They said they had been staying with a family friend and had been allowed to attend the show on their own. Somehow, they had escaped from the theater but were so shaken that they didn't know what to do. They had simply walked until they saw an open door and came into the shop.

A kind employee took them to the train station and bought them two tickets to Aurora.

Theodore Shabad, 12, had gone to the show with his 14-year-old sister, Myrtle. Though badly injured, he managed to get out of the theater and stagger eight blocks to his father's law office. Once inside, he collapsed and never woke up again. Myrtle was found dead inside the Iroquois.

Dr. D.W. Alexander's son, Boyer, was found with his head missing. He was identified by a pocket watch in his clothing. It had been a birthday gift from his father.

Myron Decker, the prosperous Chicago real estate broker, who had reluctantly attended the show at the Iroquois, even though he had a fear of theater and fires, had perished that afternoon with his wife and daughter.

What had seemed like an unnecessary fear had turned out to be a prophetic one.

Barbara Reynolds, the woman who had looked around the theater and proclaimed it a "death trap" to her sister, had also died in the fire.

Mary Dorothy Gartz, 12, and her little four-year-old sister, Jean, had attended the theater that day with their aunt, Adelaide Hopfelt. As the trio tried to escape from the building, they became separated, and Adelaide managed to make it outside with severe burns to her head and shoulders.
Mary and Jean were never seen again.

Edith Mizen, the high school junior who attended the theater that day against her parents' wishes, managed to escape unscathed. Another member of the Theta Pi Zeta Club survived with terrible burns, but all the rest of Edith's friends died in the fire.

Harry Ludwig, the manager of the Hallwood Cash Register Company, had decided to take the day off and attend the show with his wife, Sadie, and their two daughters, Caroline and Eugenie. Located near the theater, the cash register company that Harry managed opened its doors to care for at least 50 of the injured from the fire. His staff worried about him all day and feared the worst when he had not returned by evening.

And they were right - Harry, Sadie, Caroline, and Eugenie all died at the Iroquois.

The community of Kenosha was staggered by the loss of life from the fire. The members of the Henry Van Ingen family became separated as they tried to flee the theater. The parents survived with burns, but their five children - Grace, Edward, John, Margaret, and Elizabeth - all died in the flames. Henry and his wife eventually recovered from their physical injuries but were never the same emotionally. They didn't return to Kenosha. Instead, they moved to Tarrytown, New York, where they remained for the rest of their lives.

The Cooper brothers from Kenosha decided to remain in their seats instead of risking the stampede for the exits. Their bodies were found near each other. Both had suffocated from the smoke.

Charlotte Plamondon, whose father had been at the theater's opening night, and little Margaret Revell and her friend, Elizabeth Harris, all survived. Housewares merchant Alexander Revell heard about the fire while in his store, jumped into a cab, and made a fast trip to the theater. Luckily, he quickly found his daughter, her friend, and the maid who had taken them to the show, standing in the street, all unhurt. After he got them away from the scene, Revell stayed to help carry victims out of the building.

Charlotte and her entire party escaped from their box, uninjured but without coats. "The first thing we did was rush to the shops to buy wraps," she later said.

Rosamond Parrish, 19, was a student and Kappa Kappa Gamma sorority member at Wisconsin University in Madison, home for the Christmas holidays. She had decided that an afternoon matinee with friends and family was the perfect way to end her Christmas break before returning to school.

Rosamond Parrish

Her father, Charles Parrish, was a successful merchant and manufacturer. After founding a hardware and upholstery company, Gibson, Parish & Co., he turned to sheet metal fabrication. He lived with his wife, Martha, and Rosamond's four siblings, in the affluent Hyde Park neighborhood.

Rosamond perished in the fire, and after a two-day search, her remains were found at Rolston's Funeral Home.

But Rosamond had other relatives in the audience. On the first floor was her aunt Flora Parrish Tobin and two of Flora's grandsons - 11-year-old John Wright and 13-year-old

Frank Lloyd Wright, Jr. - the son of the man who would soon be one of America's greatest architects.

Stories say that Flora managed to get the two boys out of the Iroquois by sticking a hatpin into anyone who got in their way. True or not, they did make it out of the theater, even after being separated. John found himself outside the theater, feeling frightened until his father arrived, and they spotted one another.

While his father went inside to look for Lloyd and Flora, Flora escaped and met up with John. She found a telephone, called home and found that Lloyd was already there. He had borrowed cab fare from a stranger and managed to get there safe and sound.

Lula Greenwald had attended the show that day with family friend Verna Goss, Verna's mother, and her little sister, Helen. In the rush for the door, the others had gotten separated from Lula and her son, Leroy. Verna Goss and her sister escaped, but Lula and her son did not.

Two months later, a bizarre plot to steal Lula's jewelry was discovered by the Chicago police. During the confusion after the fire, a man named John Mahken concocted a scheme to hire an undertaker to bury Lula's body, which Mahken had identified as an aunt from Montreal. He had followed the corpse to a funeral home, where he identified the body, wept dramatically, and put in a claim for any valuables she had on her when she died. Mahken was still waiting to collect the jewelry when her husband had Lula's body disinterred and officially identified her as his wife after days of searching.

In Galesburg, Illinois, the family of Dorsha Hayes was safely at home, but the small town had not gotten through the tragedy unscathed. The local postmaster, F.A. Freer, had lost both his wife and his daughter, Alda, in the fire. Freer had caught the midnight fast mail train to Chicago and wired his family the next morning: "Have found Alda dead. Mamma not yet found. Will wire you later. Papa."

A registry clerk at the Chicago Post Office, Clinton Meeker, lost his wife, two sons, and two daughters in the fire. A friend had telephoned him during the afternoon and asked if the family had gone to see *Mr. Bluebeard*. Clinton said that, as far as he knew, none of them had gone anywhere. But he arrived home later that day to find only his mother-in-law there. When he asked her where Mabel and the children had gone, she replied that they had gone to the Iroquois Theater.

"I dropped right down on my knees and prayed that God might spare them," he recalled. But his prayer wasn't answered. Later that week, he identified the bodies of his wife and daughters. His sons were never found.

Ethel Blackman, 17, had attended the theater that day with her father, Harry, who worked for Marshall Field's. In the panic after the fire started, the two of them became separated. Harry managed to make it to the Randolph Street lobby, and then he went back inside to look for his daughter. He soon tragically found her burned body on a staircase.

Overcome with grief, he wrapped her in an overcoat, carried her outside, and took a taxi to the Northwestern railroad station, where he caught the first train to Glenview.

Ethel was finally home.

And he was not the only one to simply walk away with the dead. Another man, using his overcoat as a shroud, wrapped up his dead wife and carried her home to Evanston. The circumstances of her death were not known until several days later when he applied for a burial permit.

More than 24 hours after the disaster, an exhausted-looking man boarded a Cottage Grove Avenue streetcar. In his arms, partially wrapped in a piece of canvas, was the body of a little girl. As he took his seat, the conductor came over and tapped him on the shoulder. "I'm sorry," he told the man, "but the rules of the company do not permit the carrying of bodies in this manner. I must ask you to leave the car."

The man never said a word. He slowly stood, cradling the child in one arm, and with his free hand, he pulled a revolver from his pocket. He pointed it at the conductor's face. He finally spoke: "This is my daughter. I have looked for her all last night and all of today. I am taking my baby home to her mother, and I intend to take her on this car. Now go on."

The streetcar continued on its way.

A few days after the fire, a man was seen on Randolph Street, across the street from the padlocked entrance to the Iroquois. He paced back and forth in the cold and mumbled to himself. Sometimes he would sit down on the dirty curb as traffic rumbled past, look at the burned-out theater, and break out in hysterical laughter.

He had lost his wife and his children in the fire.

Over the weekend that followed, Chicago's priests, ministers, and rabbis held more than 300 funerals, each with its own story of horror and grief. In some cases, entire families were buried together. One rabbi was even said to have collapsed from exhaustion after performing 15 funerals over two days.

At Oakwoods Cemetery, the entire family of Dr. M.B. Rimes - his wife and three children - were buried in one plot.

A holiday reunion had turned to a day of horror for friends of a prominent Wheaton physician, Dr. Charles S. Owen. He and a party of 11 friends and relatives had been seated in the first row of the Iroquois' balcony. All of them were killed in the fire, and Dr. Owen himself died from his injuries just minutes after the clock announced the New Year.

Scattered throughout the audience, 14 women fainted during a triple funeral at Evanston's Second Presbyterian Church for Mrs. F.S. Butler, her son, and her adopted daughter.

The home of the Holst family was still decorated for Christmas - with a large sign proclaiming "Peace on Earth, Goodwill to Men" on the porch - when a funeral was being held for Mary Holst, her son, and two daughters, at Forest Home Cemetery. Only Mary's husband and her six-month-old son had stayed home from the theater that day.

All but five of the nearly 350 people who worked in the Mr. Bluebeard production survived. Considering how many were backstage -- and the disorganized, panicky behavior they exhibited - it's surprising that there were not more. The dead included a minor, bit-part actor Burr Scott, a 22-year-old usher, two female attendants, and aerialist Nellie Reed.

Over time, Nellie's death has been the strangest and most confusing of all those from the Iroquois fire. There are a number of contradictory reports about how she was fatally injured and what happened to her during the fire. It is possible that some of the stagehands confused Nellie with other aerialists. They were all identically costumed, right down to their blond wigs, and all of them were petite. With the darkness and smoke in the theater, it's very possible that mistaken identity might account for how many different Nellie stories there are. It also might explain an unsubstantiated account of a performer named "Floraline," who allegedly died just as the fire started. "Floraline" was also an aerial dancer, so it's possible - even likely - that her story and Nellie's story are one and the same.

What we do know is that when the fire started, Nellie was still high above the stage with the Grigolatis. One of the performers was the possibly fictitious "Floraline." She is said to have panicked and died in a fall to the stage below. Nellie, meanwhile, was forgotten and left attached to her wire.

At some point, though, she got free, and the theater's engineer, Robert Murray, said that he found her on the stage level, badly injured. She had managed to unhook herself from her wire. He said he grabbed her and took her out to the street, where he handed her to some rescuers.

At least that's one version of the Nellie Reed story.

There is another that is not as credible, but which has also been told. In this case, a stagehand named William Wietz found her in her dressing room. He claimed that she was nearly naked, so he wrapped her in his coat and attempted to get her on an elevator car. She resisted because she was afraid of the elevator and squirmed out of his reach, falling over a railing to the stage below. Wietz's story about Nellie being afraid of the elevator seems unlikely considering that she had spent at least two years before the fire helplessly suspended from wires in the air. Wietz did not describe his own descent to the stage floor to see if she'd survived the fall, and his entire story was not reported and attributed to him until 46 years after the fire.

In another version of events - this one told by Charles Bloomingdale, Jr. to the *Saturday Evening Post* in March 1904 - a chorus girl had seen Nellie unable to free herself from her harness. This young woman claimed that an elevator operator, Robert Smith, broke the ropes connected to Nellie's harness and freed her to escape. There were some reports about Smith dragging some of the performers out of their dressing rooms during the fire, but nothing was reported in the Chicago newspapers about him breaking harness ropes.

Was there any truth in these alternate stories? Robert Murray testified that he had found Nellie hysterical, in great pain and incoherent, scratching against a wall. He had gotten her out of the theater using a coal chute. Could she have fallen from the staircase before he found her, as Wietz claimed? It seems unlikely, but I suppose it is possible.

What we do know beyond that is that Nellie was treated for burns and smoke inhalation at Cook County Hospital, but she died a few days later. Her body was shipped to New York for a funeral on January 3.

And that's all we know for sure.

There is a story that claims that while performing together in *Sleeping Beauty and the Beast*, Nellie became close friends with actress Viola Gillette. It was reported that Viola paid for Nellie's funeral expenses and planned for her to be buried in Viola's lot in the famous Green-Wood Cemetery in Brooklyn, New York.

A funeral service was held for Nellie in New York City on Friday, January 8, at the Stephen Merritt Embalming Institute on West 23rd Street. Reverend Homer Taylor of the Church of the Holy Communion read the Episcopal burial service, and a double quartet of members from *Sleeping Beauty* and *Mother Goose* stage companies sang hymns.

After that, Nellie Reed vanished from history.

No one knows where she was buried. Some say her body was returned to England, and others claim she was buried

FUNERAL OF NELLIE REED.

Funeral services over the remains of Nellie Reed, the ballet girl of the Mr. Bluebeard company, who died from injuries received in the Iroquois Theatre fire, were held at the Stephen Merritt undertaking establishment, in this city, on last Friday afternoon. The Rev. Homer Taylor, of the Church of the Holy Communion, read the Episcopal burial service, and a double quartette, composed of members of The Sleeping Beauty and the Beast and The Mother Goose companies, sang the hymns. Many professional people were present, including all of the members of the Mr. Bluebeard company, who have returned from Chicago. The floral tributes were many and beautiful. Viola Gillette, Miss Reed's foster sister, made all arrangements for the funeral, and in case Miss Reed's uncle, who lives in England, has no wish to the contrary, the remains will be buried in Miss Gillette's plot in Greenwood Cemetery.

in Brooklyn, as Viola Gillette had planned. If she was buried there, however, there is no record of it. Green-Wood does have extensive burial listings but officials there admit they are not complete.

It just seems to be another mystery in the life and death of aerialist Nellie Reed.

Eddie Foy became known internationally overnight. Virtually every account of the fire mentioned his name and included all or part of his story of trying to stop the panic in the auditorium.

Like many members of the company, Eddie had suffered burns and minor injuries, but he felt that it was a miracle that so few members of the theater company had died. He stated this in testimony before a special investigative committee and in an oddly worded note dated January 5, 1904. It had been perhaps written to one of the cast members and read: "The catastrophe at the Iroquois was a miracle. It considered it a perfect theater and I don't think that from the time the fire started till the stampede took place and people were smothered in the gallery, could not have exceeded ninety seconds... It was not a fire but a miracle."

But the people of Chicago did not consider the disaster a "miracle." The Iroquois fire crowded out every other event in the city on the front pages of the newspapers. They detailed the changing casualty figures. They revealed photos of the theater's scorched interior and police officers and fire officials standing next to exit doors, where the greatest loss of life occurred. There were artist's sketches of the fire as it spread and tragic images of many of the victims, especially the children.

Mayor Harrison issued a string of executive orders, first closing all the theaters and places of public amusement except for the Chicago Auditorium, which had a steel fire curtain. He closed dime museums, dance halls, and other public buildings, including some hospitals. All were shut down until proper safety inspections could take place.

Someone, the public cried, had to answer for the fire, and a coroner's inquest was launched to determine the exact cause of the fire. A special committee of architects and builders was also appointed to interview survivors and report directly to the mayor.

But despite these quick responses - and assurances of improvements to public safety in the city - the public wasn't satisfied. Mayor Harrison soon found himself in the center of a controversy that would eventually end his political career.

11. THE FINGER POINTING BEGINS

Blame for the Iroquois Theater Fire would first and foremost be blamed on Mayor Carter Harrison, Jr., but he certainly did not bear the brunt of it alone. The real blame can be traced back to years before the fire occurred and can be found deep in Chicago's long history of corruption.

Mayor Harrison was just the most convenient target in 1903 and 1904.

Weeks before the theater had even opened, investigative journalist Lincoln Steffens had written a series of articles about corruption in the city. He painted a very damning picture of Chicago as Carter Harrison was running it.

In one article, he noted:

> *It is absurdly backward and uneven; the fire department is excellent, the police is a disgrace, the law department is expert, the health bureau is corrupt, and the street cleaning is hardly worth mention.*
>
> *All this is Carter H. Harrison. He is an honest man personally, but indolent; a shrewd politician, and a character with reserve power, but he has no initial energy. Without ideals, he does not know what is demanded of him. He does not seem to know wrong is wrong, till he is taught, nor to car, till criticism arouses his political sense of popular requirement. But think of it, every time Chicago wants to go ahead a foot, it has to push its mayor up inch by inch. In brief, Chicago is a city that wants to be led, and Carter Harrison, with all his political ambition, honest willingness, and obstinate independence, simply follows it."*

Corruption had long been the lifeblood of Chicago. One of the great eras for vice, prostitution, liquor, and gambling in the city had been during the five terms of office held by

Mayor Carter Harrison, Sr. - father of the mayor at the time of the Iroquois disaster.

His fifth election campaign was largely funded by collections from gamblers across the city. After the election, Harrison returned the favor by forming a syndicate to collect a fixed percentage of his profits from every gambler and confidence man. This would range from 40- to 65-percent, in return for which they were guaranteed protection against interference by the police. During the 1893 World's Fair, this fund amounted to a large fortune. And even though several people dipped their fingers into the pie before the money reached Harrison, the mayor still managed to pocket a rather tidy sum.

Harrison had promised during his campaign that he would give visitors to the World's Fair a "wide-open town," and he more than kept his word. Until he was assassinated on October 19, 1893, by a disgruntled office-seeker, Chicago was probably the most wide-open town that America had ever seen - and the most corrupt. Everyone in Chicago who was capable of common sense knew that all the city government departments reeked of graft and bribery, but no one felt compelled to do anything about it. It was a way of life in Chicago. It had always been that way, and no one attempted to change it aside from a few would-be reformers.

During the second Carter Harrison term in office, graft continued. Police, alderman, building inspectors, and others followed Harrison's hands-off attitude. "Boodling," a slang term for payoffs, frequently appeared in the papers. Bookmaking was openly carried out in corner cigar stores. An Illinois state law ordered all saloons to be closed on Sundays - but not in Chicago, where Harrison didn't enforce it. The city allowed a segregated Red Light District to flourish. It became such a colorful part of the city that the two sisters that ran the notorious and elegant Everleigh Club published and distributed an elaborate guidebook with photographs that featured everything bordello had to offer.

The newspapers, despite the critical editorials that frequently appeared, quietly went along with all of it. For example, the Tribune ran a lengthy "war on vice" in its pages and specifically attacked the Everleigh sisters, but office clerks at the paper who needed to find late-night reporters in a hurry were instructed to first call the Everleigh Club to track them down. Reporters treated the "nightly shootings, robberies, kidnappings, and occasional scandals involving playboys" that occurred in Chicago's First Ward as "amusing recreational reading."

In 1903, the press corps numbered nearly 600 and were not held in very high regard by the mayor, who was often criticized and ridiculed in the various local dailies.

Mayor Harrison, who earned $833 a month, was not less critical of most of the city's aldermen. Their monthly stipend was $125, but most were also saloonkeepers, owners of gambling houses, and entrenched in the city's vice districts

- often referring to them as a "motley crew" and "gangsters."

Among the worst to thrive during this era were Michael "Hinky-Dink" Kenna and "Bathhouse" John Coughlin, who ran the notorious, crime-infested First Ward, starting in the late 1890s. They made a legendary team, collecting graft and doling out favors in the area to those who paid the most. In 1911, when Mayor Harrison gave the word to Captain Patrick J. Harding to order his divisional inspector John Wheeler to close the famed Everleigh Club brothel, the inspector did nothing until he received the okay from aldermen Kenna and Coughlin.

Notorious Chicago aldermen, Michael "Hinky-Dink" Kenna and "Bathhouse" John Coughlin

Coughlin was known as "Bathhouse" because he had once been a masseur in a Turkish bath. He was a large, poetry-spouting buffoon known for being outgoing and good-hearted and a bizarre dresser, sporting garishly colored waistcoats. His poetry often appeared in Chicago newspapers, and after hearing some of his public statements, many mistook him for being simple-minded. Mayor Harrison once asked his partner, Kenna, if Bathhouse was crazy or taken with drugs. Kenna replied that he was neither. "To tell you the God's truth, Mayor, they ain't found a name for it yet."

Kenna was Coughlin's mirror opposite. He was small, glum, and quietly dressed and was known for being shrewd and close-mouthed. At Kenna's Workingman's Exchange on Clark Street, patrons were served what was referred to as the "Largest and Coolest Schooner of Beer in the City" and the best free lunch around, too. There were no orchestras here, no women, no music, and no selling to minors. Here, for more than 20 years, the bums, the homeless, and the jobless of the First Ward ate and drank for a nickel. Kenna also found jobs for the down and out and often rescued them from trouble with the police.

But he also told them how to vote, and he never lost an election or primary. He and Bathhouse created this astonishing record by marshaling the ward's party workers on Election Day to get votes from railroad hands, tramps, thieves, and any other warm bodies that were available. They were taken to a polling place and were given already marked ballots that were deposited in a box. When they returned with the unmarked ballots -- taken from the polling place -- they could turn them in for a fee of 50-cents. Those ballots were then marked and used at another polling place, where the whole scheme was repeated.

The two men made an unlikely pair but were a highly effective and increasingly wealthy duo. In addition to the other services they offered, such as guaranteed voting in the First Ward, they also provided protection for various illicit enterprises. They exacted regular and weekly tributes that ranged from $25 per week from the small brothels and as much as $100 from the larger ones. They received an additional fee if drinks were sold, or gambling occurred there. They also offered fees for legal work as well, such as stopping indictments for charges of grand larceny, pandering, theft, or kidnapping. These fees could range from $500 to $2,000.

They were able to provide such services thanks to the fact that Coughlin and Kenna had men who were beholden to them in every municipal, county, state, and federal office in the city. They controlled the jobs of city workers, including inspectors and the police, and were also, as aldermen, in a position to grant favors to respectable businessmen in Chicago. They could usually count on a routine take of between $15,000 and $30,000 per year. Special votes that were purchased bought them in anywhere from $8,000 to $100,000 each, depending on the importance of the matter. The two men went carefully about their business filling the requests that the financiers of Chicago were willing to pay for, such as zoning variances, permits, tax deductions, licenses, and other amenities.

It was constantly, and justifiably, assumed by the public that the two of them were corrupt, although nothing was ever proven against them. Their most famous exploit was an annual party, and it was such an outstanding example of public debauchery that it was eventually shut down.

The First Ward Ball, which they organized, was referred to as an "annual underworld orgy." It was required that every prostitute, pimp, pickpocket, and thief buy at least one ticket, while the owners of brothels and saloons had to purchase large blocks of them. The madams usually had their own boxes, where they could rub shoulders with city officials and politicians. The First Ward Ball grew larger every year until the two aldermen were making as much as $50,000 from it. They held the ball at the Chicago Coliseum. After one spectacle, the *Chicago Tribune* wrote, "If a great disaster had befallen the Coliseum last night, there would not have been a second story worker, a dip or pug ugly, porch climber, dope fiend or scarlet woman remaining in Chicago."

But members of the press and reformers in the city believed that the corruption of aldermen like "Bathhouse" John and "Hinky Dink" Kenna, among others, reflected Harrison's own ineptitude. As Edgar Lee Masters recalled, "Nearly everything was a lie in the city. Harrison believed the vices could not be eradicated and they could only be driven from one cover to another and in the face of numerous reform committees, who implored him to enforce the law, he let the city have as it would, concerning himself with order and proper protections of the citizens."

However, when Harrison permitted the Iroquois Theater to open when it did, the mayor seemed to have ignored the "proper protection" of everyone who walked through its doors.

Thanks to the long-running feud between Harrison and most of the city's aldermen, the tragic consequences of the Iroquois fire were set in motion nearly two months before the theater opened. At the time, the mayor charged that "petty grafting and wholesale grafting were rife in every Chicago municipal department." It was a sensational charge - even if most people assumed it was accurate. Harrison told the press, "If I could fire all the men I suspect of grafting, they would all be jumping out every window in City Hall. This hall is full of graft big and little. You know it and can't prove it. I've got 18 months left, and I'll get some of them yet."

In the wake of the fire, the mayor accused aldermen of not acting on the critical study that had been submitted by the building's commission about the failure of safety measures in the city's theater two months before the Iroquois opened. Harrison said that "if anyone was to blame for the fire, they were." Aldermen had suspended action on a new city ordinance for theaters because the report needed further "examination." On October 19, the city council had ordered: "that any action against the theater violations be stayed until the judiciary committee reported on the amended ordinance." A resolution was passed calling on the mayor to name three aldermen who, together with the city engineer and building commissioner, would make up a committee that would draft new ordinances for theater construction and report back to the council in three weeks.

Harrison claimed that he did submit a document to the council on November 2, eight weeks before the fire, but said that it was referred back to the judiciary committee, which, at the time the fire occurred, had "practically agreed upon amending ordinances, giving time for theaters to comply." Since they didn't take immediate action, Mayor Harrison said, the city council - not the mayor - was responsible for the disaster.

Box office employees at other theaters blamed the "Free List" for the hundreds of deaths at the Iroquois. These were tickets commonly given out by Chicago theaters that were "constructed and conducted in violation of municipal laws." In other words, they were tickets given away for free so that inspectors looked the other way when there were problems at the theater. This was a widespread practice - no surprise there - in Chicago.

In a statement issued to newspapers, theater owners Davis and Powers rushed to provide their own implausible excuse. They said that when the fire started, the house fireman "threw the contents of the Kilfyre, which would have been more than enough, if the product had been effective, to have extinguished the flame at once, but for some cause inherent in the tube of Kilfyre, it had no effect."

The claim that the Kilfyre failed to work was immediately challenged by one alderman who said the theater's management had been explicitly warned about the inadequacy of the product after a member of his staff, a veteran fireman, had visited the theater. One day before the tragedy, the alderman said, the former firefighter warned a member of the theater's management that the "fire apparatus you have here would do no more good than a bucket of water in a sawmill." But the man was told to mind his own business - he was not in charge of the theater."

That was bad enough, but Davis and Powers weren't done yet. Next, they topped things off by blaming the victims. "The audience was promptly admonished and importuned by persons on the stage and in the auditorium to be calm and avoid any rush." They added that "the exits and facilities for emptying the theater were ample to enable them all to get out without confusion." And then ended the statement with, "no expense or precaution was omitted to make the theater as fireproof as it could be made, there being nothing combustible in the construction of the house except the trimmings and furnishings of the stage, and in building the theater we sacrificed more space to aisles and exits than any theatre in America."

In an example of both poor timing and bad taste, Will Davis' wife, the actress, and singer Jessie Bartlett Davis chimed in from Philadelphia, where she was performing. She also blamed the victims for the disaster, claiming that it was the actors whose lives were regularly in danger. "It is the fault of the public that such things occur," she said. "In these swift days, the public is not satisfied with good, quiet shows. They must have lots of excitement, color, and light, with the result that every actor takes his life in his hands when he goes before the footlights."

Jessie's comments were already questionable but then she took things one step further. She added, "I do not understand how the asbestos curtain failed to work. Mrs. Davis drilled his men every day in the use of the apparatus and in the dropping of the curtain. Never before was there any hitch."

But the curtain itself was the hitch.

Most agreed that there was no way that the curtain that Powers had purchased had been a pure asbestos curtain. If it had been, said the local manager of the Johns-Manville Company, it would have "stood the test" of the Iroquois fire. The company was quick to distance itself from the tragedy. They took out prominent ads in theatrical papers stating, "Asbestos curtains that stop fires are pure asbestos interwoven with brass wire. The Iroquois Theater curtain was not one of ours."

Gustave J. Johnson, a chemist and member of the Western Society of Engineers, stated firmly that the curtain at the Iroquois was "not asbestos at all." Powers had replaced the costly asbestos curtain with a much cheaper one. Johnson had examined fabric from the curtain after the fire and found that while it did contain a small amount of asbestos, "it was largely wood pulp. By mixing pulp with asbestos fiber, the life of the curtain is prolonged, the cost is cheapened, and the wire foundation can be dispensed with... It results in a curtain that may get inside city ordinances but is of no value in a fire."

Chicago fire insurance underwriters accused the city of failing to comply with established building ordinances and failing to enforce them. This was not, the underwriters stated, the insurance industry's responsibility.

The Iroquois, it turned out, was not insured.

The theater's architect, Benjamin Marshall, was on a business trip to Pittsburgh when the fire occurred, and he caught the first train back to Chicago. Shocked by what had happened, he was baffled by the loss of life because there had been so many available exits.

He had no idea that most of them had been locked by the theater's management.

Marshall did say that, in the future, he planned to stop using lavish interior wood trim and heavy, flammable curtains in his designs. Foolishly, he defended using heavy drapes to hide the exit doors because it "improved the interior look" of the new theater. He added that in his design, there had been an electrical switch near the office that could have turned on the auditorium lights - but the staff was unaware of its location.

The Klaw and Erlanger organization was also blamed, especially for importing the highly combustible scenery from England. They were also accused of disregarding the safety of their patrons by violating city fire regulations. *Life* magazine mentioned Klaw and Erlanger by name in the caption for a cartoon showing the skeletal figure of death holding the keys and standing in front of the locked entrance to the Iroquois as the hands of victims tried to open the doors. They sued the magazine for libel, but the case was tossed out of court.

Chief Musham was blamed for not demanding that house fireman Sallers inform him that the theater's fire apparatus was incomplete. In his defense, Musham said that although he did not require Sallers to report to him about the safety equipment, it had been Sallers' responsibility to do so. Captain "Paddy" Jennings had predicted that Sallers would be lynched if people found out how ill-prepared the theater was for a fire. It wasn't happening literally, but he was being "lynched" all the same.

As arguments and finger-pointing continued, the fire department's attorney, Monroe Fulkerson, started his own investigation, and Coroner Traeger prepared for an inquest involving hundreds of witnesses. He promised that those responsible would be brought to justice.

But they wouldn't be.

Almost everyone connected to the Iroquois was blamed for something. Local unions blamed the theater management for taking advantage of layoffs by the Fuller Construction Company to save money hiring unskilled workers. The Chicago Federation of Labor said the theater had refused to hire well-paid, experienced workmen, pointing to the fact

The skylights of the Iroquois had been nailed shut at the time of the fire, preventing them from venting out smoke and flames through the roof. On the day after the fire, employees of Fuller Construction snuck onto the roof and removed the boards before city officials could inspect them

that William McMullen, the operator of the light that caused the fire, was just "learning the trade."

Oliver Sollett, one of the city's biggest contractors, said that "bribery and graft were responsible, that in addition to the theater having no place to emit smoke and fumes, that chairs were placed where specifications called for aisles." He also said that exits were too small to allow patrons to escape.

The Fuller Company was blamed for, among other things, not finishing work on the equipment that controlled the skylights above the stage - which would have vented out most of the smoke and flames through the roof instead of sending it into the balcony and gallery - and leaving the skylights nailed shut.

These were serious accusations and were made worse when the contractor tried to tamper with evidence. On the day after the fire, while police officers and Pinkerton detectives surrounded the building, Fuller workers got onto the theater's roof from another building and removed the boards that sealed off the skylights before city inspectors, and other officials could examine them.

This illegal action caused a statement issued by Fuller's local manager, W.A. Merriman, to not exactly ring true. Even though Merriman had lost his wife and three-year-old daughter in the fire, he had the nerve to say, "The Iroquois Theater was built with safety as the first consideration. All the building ordinances were adhered to in every detail. I do not hesitate to state that there was no theater building in the country which was freer from danger. The exits were numerous and all the work our company performed was absolutely fireproof. After making a careful inspection since the fire, I find that the structure, as erected, still stands."

It was true that the building was still standing, but the fact that hundreds had died because the ventilation system had not been completed and the fire escapes had not been attached could hardly be ignored.

The press - and not just in Chicago - unanimously condemned the owners of the theater and city officials.

Harrison's closing of the other theaters in the city was criticized as too little, too late.

One day after the fire, the *Chicago Tribune* wrote:

> *The theater had just been built and inspected. It had been built by artisans whom, in our moments of national pride, we call the cleverest in the world. It has been inspected by officials whom recent public indignation was supposed to have awakened to some sense of public duty. It was a modern building, constructed with modern requirements. It was said, and it was supposed to be fact, that the building was not only a fireproof one but that every device which ingenuity, spurred by a desire to guard human life, could think of had been installed - that abundant precautions were taken and that the theater, at least, was safe. Yet, that is the theater which had gained a terrible celebrity.*
>
> *The dead cannot be called to life, but the other theaters of Chicago can be inspected in light of the dread illumination of the Iroquois fire.*

Mayor Harrison tried to deflect criticism of his administration and the theater's management by choosing certain aldermen to make speeches that urged public calm and moderation at the first city council meeting after the fire. But the *Inter-Ocean*, as well as other papers, called the tactic "futile" and "craven." The mayor could say anything he wanted; editorials written by Harrison would be "judged, censured, and condemned" by the dead.

The *Chicago Tribune* continued to call for the city administration and its "incapable and corrupt servants" to take some responsibility for the disaster. The paper also demanded that the theater's managers take their share of the blame. "Nor can the owners, architect, and builders of the theater be acquitted in the public mind of a full share of responsibility."

The *New York Times*, whose readers included some of the most powerful names on Broadway, asked, "How does it come to pass that so many, or any, theaters could open their doors and do business month after month under conditions of such obvious violation of the law that a casual inspection would discover the fact? Is this official malfeasance or ordinary graft? The trouble is less with the law than with laxness in its enforcement, and the persons primarily responsible for the Chicago horror are the city officials of Chicago."

Life magazine chimed in again to state the obvious: "The Iroquois was new and was called fireproof. This is a story of a cheap asbestos curtain that would not come down, of exits and fire escapes by which people could not get out, of laws not enforced and precautions neglected - a dismal story of preventable disaster."

The religious leaders of Chicago were also outraged. The tragedy had angered many usually mild-mannered clergymen, and they were speaking out on behalf of their angry, confused, and frightened parishioners.

"Chicago is in the hands of a government of monkeys," declared Reverend Franklyn Johnson of the University of Chicago. "It is ridiculous for those men in office to spring up now with the cry of 'punish the guilty' while they are the guilty ones. It is time for intelligent people to wake up and see in whose hands the safety of their lives is entrusted."

Bishop Samuel Fallows, who had carried out the dead from the Iroquois with his own hands, stated that the authorities should "let no guilty man escape."

During a funeral for two children, Rabbi Moses Perez Jacobson called the fire "one of the great calamities of the age." Another rabbi at a memorial service added, "This fire was not an act of God but due to criminal ignorance, neglect, and recklessness."

Mayor Harrison was being attacked from all sides, including by dozens of newspapers running front-page cartoons almost every day that lampooned him as a buffoon. He tried to respond to public pressure, but his actions were loaded with political and economic consequences no matter what he did. When he closed all the theaters, he put 6,000 performers and theater employees out of work for the first two weeks of 1904. With almost all the theaters dark, business leaders - especially downtown restaurant owners - became alarmed at the prospect of empty stores and eateries.

When business leaders went to City Hall to try and urge the mayor to withdraw or at least postpone the closure order, they received what they described as "a frosty reception." Harrison simply informed them that other public places would soon be closed, including dance halls, churches, office buildings, and department stores.

Meanwhile, the police started making arrests. They began with 20 stagehands, carpenters, and even some of the "Pale Moonlight" singers, some of whom were charged with involuntary manslaughter. The singers were held on a technicality so they could serve as witnesses. Theater owners Davis and Powers were also arrested.

Judge George Underwood issued the arrest warrants at the insistence of Arthur Hull, the Chicago businessman who had been unable to attend the show because of his work duties but arranged it as a surprise for his wife and children.

All of them had died in the disaster.

Hull spoke out to the newspapers about his personal tragedy, and his heartbreaking words appeared on front pages across the country. Even in his despair over the loss of his family, he was skeptical of the arrests that had been made:

It is too terrible to contemplate. I can never go to my home again. To look at playthings left by the children just where they put them, to see how my dear dead wife arranged the details of her home so carefully, the very walls ring with the names of my dear dead ones. I can never go there again.

My wife and children, all I ever had to live for, are gone. All that remains is for me to try and make someone pay for this carelessness. A few carpenters and stagehands have been arrested. Men who sang in the chorus are in jail. Such an investigation is a cruel mockery. The men who are responsible are allowed to walk the streets untouched while a few laborers are punished. The authorities must understand that those who have suffered will not wait for them to dally along. There must be no politics or favoritism in this investigation.

It wasn't just Arthur Hull and other survivors who were paying attention to the workings of the city's government. The press was also watching, and when Mayor Harrison and members of the city council toured the burned-out theater on January 1, reporters followed close behind and photographed the inspection.

City officials and police officers toured the Iroquois to see the disaster for themselves. They were shocked and appalled by what they saw – especially because so many people were blaming the authorities for the terrible loss of life

With the exception of the basement, where firefighters were still pumping out water, and the police were searching in vain for more bodies, the mayor walked through the entire building. The place was crowded with photographers who shot everything from the ruined stage to the locked gates and doors where so many people had died, the blistered walls, the blackened floors, and the devastation of the auditorium.

Architect Benjamin Marshall accompanied Harrison on the tour. At one point, the mayor noted the failure to comply with the city ordinance that required exits to be marked with printed signs. He also asked why so many of the doors had been covered with curtains. Marshall's response about improving the appearance of the house was not well-received, nor was his explanation that the exit signs were "being made, but temporary signs were not being used because it was not desired to mar the beauty of the interior with them."

This stupid reply got an immediate - and very angry - response from one of the aldermen, who said, "This theater was opened on November 23. It has been running fully five weeks. In heaven's name, how long does it take to make signs?"

It is possible Marshall may have actually been that ignorant. Reporter Charles Collins reported on an element of the architect's plans that, if true, was both revealing and disturbing. In Marshall's plan, the same staircase reached both the main auditorium and the first and second balconies. This violated Chicago city ordinances that required both balconies have separate stairways and street entrances. Ignoring these regulations was a fatal error - many lives could have been saved if the upper parts of the house could have exited using their own stairways rather than having to fight through a crush of people converging on the same landing from different parts of the theater.

Collins learned that the single grand staircase was designed to appeal to the class-consciousness of usual theatergoers. This was reinforced by a sentence in the opening night program that Collins took home as a souvenir:

"To see and be seen is the duality of advantage presented for patrons of the Iroquois."

Collins recalled that phrase - "to see and be seen" - had been used by Marshall when he showed off the theater on opening night. While standing with a group of friends, he said, "Do you notice that sections of the first and second balconies enter by the same marble staircase? The purchasers of cheap seats will look just as prosperous as the others when they go up those stairs, and people like it better than to have to go outside and enter by separate entrances. Then, when friends see them coming down the marble steps, they did not know whether they came from the first or second balcony."

Apart from only appealing to snobs, the design elements of the balcony promenade and grand staircase were confusing, especially in a panicked situation - like a fire, for instance. Coming out of the balcony was a promenade that extended around the foyer. To go down to the lobby, balcony patrons first had to walk up four steps, turn left, and then descend a grand staircase. The wall near the top of the staircase was confusing, too. While it appeared to be a double door, one-half of it was actually mirrored glass on a fixed wooden frame.

As newspapers across the country wrote about the terrible conditions of the Iroquois Theater, Klaw and Erlanger did all they could to distance themselves from a theater that had just recently been described as their "crown jewel." They complained about the newspapers' coverage, which suggested they were somehow to blame when the fault was clearly that of Will Davis and Harry Powers, stockholders and resident managers of the house. In a letter they added, "We believe that when calmer counsel prevails and the proper investigation is completed, it will be found that nothing was left undone that could have been foreseen to safeguard the public from that lamentable disaster."

The press, however, refused to accept any defensive arguments from city officials and theater owners. It was simple. As prominent architect Robert S. Lindstrom stated, "every theater in Chicago is virtually a death trap."

It would be against this backdrop of anger, fear, grief, accusation, denial, and contradiction that Chicago would witness one of the strangest, most emotional, and dramatic legal battles in its history.

12. CORONER'S INQUEST

The inquest into the tragic events at the Iroquois Theater began on the cold morning of January 7, 1904, at Chicago's City Hall. It was expected to last for six days, and at least 200 witnesses were expected to testify. A team of stenographers would carefully record their words.

Among those summoned to appear were female cast members of *Mr. Bluebeard*, who had been arrested to compel their testimony. The ladies had been furnished bonds that secured their temporary release. The male members of the group remained behind bars, but not for much longer.

The cast members were alone. They had been abandoned in the city by the rest of the troupe. On Sunday, January 3, six days before the show's run in Chicago would have ended and the company disbanded, nearly the entire rest of the troupe had boarded a train for New York. All of them were downcast, and nearly all were destitute.

But it could have been worse - in the baggage car was the white coffin that contained the body of Nellie Reed.

Mrs. Ogden Armour of the Chicago meatpacking family donated $500 for the dancers in the show to settle hotel bills, but most of the young women had lost clothing and personal items, and all needed money for food. Each of them was given the money they were owed, which was a half-week's pay, but that didn't get them far. Luckily, Klaw and Erlanger offered them one-way transportation back to New York. After that, they were on their own.

The rest of those summoned to appear at the inquest were a mixed lot. Members of the audience who showed no outward physical signs of injury were seated next to those with terrible burns or were swathed in bandages. Wealthy and socially important families shared benches with actors, theater officials, uniformed police officers, grieving families, building inspectors, dancers, stagehands, firefighters, and domestic servants. The room was filled with people from every level of Chicago society, and they waited together until they were called to be questioned, one by one, in the city council chamber.

Coroner Traeger was among the city officials who toured the theater after the fire so he could better understand the conditions of the building

(Left) Coroner John Traeger

The press, of course, was also present. Reporters scratched in notebooks, and photographers carried around their bulky cameras and flash pans.

Coroner John Traeger and a six-man panel heard a litany of vivid, brave, cowardly, and terrible accounts. Many of them were contradictory. Some stagehands claimed, for instance, that it was the explosion of a backstage calcium light tank filled with hydrogen that caused the fire. The stage manager insisted that the flames shot out from an electrical switchboard, although there's no way he could have known that since he wasn't even on stage when the fire first broke out. Some said that a spark from a short circuit in the carbon arc lamp started the blaze, while others said that a gust of wind had moved a curtain against the light. Some swore that it wasn't a curtain that burned but a piece of gauze. Some witnesses testified that it was not the swinging light reflector, but the wire used for Nellie Reed's aerial ballet that blocked the closing of the fire curtain. A few audience members claimed that what came down was not the fire curtain, but the main stage drop.

There was also conflicting testimony about the ushers. Some said they refused to unlock the exit doors, some said they all fled at the first sign of trouble, and some maintained that the ushers had stayed at their posts. The backstage elevator boy was accused of being the first person to flee the building, but Eddie Foy and many of the chorus girls called him a hero. Eddie even contradicted himself, at first telling reporters that he was just offstage in the wings and saw the fire start, but then testifying that he was in his dressing room at the time, getting ready for the next act.

Even the death toll was disputed. The coroner's official list contained 565 names. A previous police report of 591 dead was declared inaccurate because of the moving of bodies from one morgue to another. The figure eventually rose to 602 - but the exact count will always be in question.

In the midst of all this, the attorney hired by the fire department, Monroe Fulkerson, had started an investigation of his own, and it had turned up some startling testimony. The theater's business manager, Thomas Noonan, a man who had previously escaped notice by everyone else, admitted to Fulkerson that, even though it was his responsibility, he had never instructed the employees under him about what to do in case of fire. He had also never assigned anyone to manage the fire apparatus. He admitted that the two ground-floor exits on Randolph Street were locked and that the north fire exits - three each from the orchestra section and the first and second balcony floors - were bolted. Noonan also admitted he had never discussed how to prevent loss of life during a panic with any of the ushers. He said that he "assumed the head usher knew his business." All he ever told house fireman Sallers was to "comply with city ordinances."

Attorney for the Chicago Fire Department, Monroe Fulkerson

When asked about the operation of the roof ventilators, Noonan replied that there were three men in charge of the equipment - the head usher, the house electrician, and the building's engineer. But head usher George Dusenberry denied responsibility. "My duties were in the auditorium," he said. "The ventilators are worked from the stage." Both the electrician and engineer said they had been given no authority to operate either the ventilators or the skylights.

Monroe Fulkerson said that Noonan's testimony was the single most crucial piece of evidence that his investigation had turned up because it clearly showed "incompetence and negligence." And he found other evidence of what he called "gross neglect." According to 15 witnesses who worked on the stage, "they never received orders from the management as to what to do in case of fire. There was never a fire drill in the theater, nor was any of the stagehands informed as to the location or use of the fire apparatus and the operation of the ventilators over the auditorium and stage."

As Fulkerson concluded, "Everything which should *not* have been done was done apparently, and things which *should* have been done were left undone."

As the coroner's inquest was just beginning, there was a "deluge" of lawsuits filed against the theater, its management, and the city of Chicago.

The first of many to follow was, seeking $10,000 in damages, was filed by Ivy Owens, the administrator of the estate of Amy Owens, one of the schoolteachers who was killed, and her mother, Mrs. Francis Owens. The city's liability immediately became an issue since the theater's management admitted that it was unlikely that they would be able to pay for the lives that had been lost. If $10,000 were paid for each person who died, they argued, they'd be liable for $6 million - money they didn't have. But lawyers who were versed in personal damage law said that it was doubtful the Owens family would receive payment from the city for death or injury on property the city didn't own. Another attorney added that "a city could not be held in damages for failure to enforce its ordinances."

So, if the city and the theater weren't going to pay for their incompetence and negligence, who was? Attorneys who filed the suits on behalf of the dead wanted an answer to that question. These lawyers were allowed to attend the coroner's proceedings but were barred from questioning witnesses. A state's attorney and his assistant were also present to gather evidence for a grand jury investigation after the coroner had completed his inquest.

But that inquest was far from over, stretching past the scheduled six days.

William Sallers testified that the theater opened before it was finished, a fact that was now well-known and corroborated by others who said city building inspectors ignored fire codes and allowed the theater to open because they'd received "complimentary tickets" from the management. When he was asked about fire protection, Sallers told the panel, "There were no buckets filled with water, no casks of water, no pumps of any description or portable fire extinguishers or pike poles."

Sallers was asked if he had told the theater owners that these things would be needed. He was, after all, the house fireman, so wasn't that part of his responsibilities?

But he replied, "No, sir, I did not. I presumed they would know what was needed in the way of fire extinguishers. He said that he had informed the business manager and Noonan had told him, "the theater management would attend to that when the house was completed, the plumbing all connected up and so forth."

On January 15, the *Inter-Ocean* was at it again. Chicago's Republican newspaper wanted the Democratic mayor's head on a pike and was determined to take down as many administration members along with him. The newspaper announced that the fire department was given a "terrific shaking up" thanks to revelations at the inquest about the department's incompetence and its lack of a system to make sure that buildings are equipped with fire appliances and follow city ordinances. It added that this might result "in the severing of a number of official heads - Fire Marshal Musham, Assistant Fire Marshal Campion, John Hannon, Chief of First Battalion, and other members of the department, who showed astonishing ignorance of their requirements and duties. They seemed to be under the impression that they were only required to 'fight flames' and appeared surprised that the public expected their department to take every precaution to prevent fire from starting and even commanded to do so by city ordinances."

The editorial about their testimony concluded, "Every effort was made by their witnesses to shift the responsibility for fire appliances to the building department."

Of the fire department command members, though, Musham bore the brunt of the attack.

Deputy Coroner Major Lawrence Buckley was particularly tough on the fire marshal, who sat in the witness chair with one arm casually draped over the brass rail of the speaker's table as if he didn't have a care in the world.

Buckley asked him, "Did you ever confer with the building department or with the board of underwriters with reference to anything pertaining to theaters or enforcements of the ordinances as they stood on the books?"

"No," Musham replied.

When the coroner asked him whether he knew a fire marshal needed to confer on those things, Musham answered, "I don't think it is."

At one point, Coroner Traeger read aloud Section 165 of the Building Ordinance, which mandated that sprinklers and other devices be approved by the board of underwriters, the building commissioner, and the fire marshal. He asked Musham if he had ever read that section, and Musham said that he had.

"Do you comply with it in reference to the Iroquois Theater?" Traeger asked him.

"I didn't think it had anything to do with the Iroquois Theater," Musham shrugged.

"Do you consider it to be your duty when, in the wisdom of the city council, they approve of an ordinance insisting on having sprinklers and appliances of that kind in the theater building, to see they are enforced?"

Musham shook his head. "I have no authority under the ordinance. That would be encroaching on another department."

"Do you consider you were doing your duty in not knowing that any theaters did not have these sprinklers, hose, or apparatus for putting out fire?"

"I consider I did my duty in this particular case because I was never notified," the fire marshal insisted. "I have nothing to say about it other than when I have been officially notified to approve of the appliances."

Musham admitted that he was aware that firemen appointed to theaters were required to report to him once a week, but when he was asked the inevitable follow-up question, "Did the firemen appointed or selected by the Iroquois Theater report to you weekly?" he replied that, "No, he didn't report to me any time."

"Why didn't you insist on his doing that?"

"Well, I don't know if I can answer that."

When pressed for an answer, Musham had to admit that he was "not at all familiar with these different ordinances." He also admitted that he didn't know that the ordinances allowed him to close theaters that didn't follow the city's standards.

Keep in mind, these were the *fire* ordinances, and he was the top fire official in the city.

Battalion Chief Hannon didn't make the fire department look any more competent. He testified that he had visited the theater in later December, weeks after it had opened, and had noticed that "the necessary precautions had not been taken." Why hadn't he reported this to his superiors?

Because no one had ordered him to do so.

A week after his own questionable testimony, William Sallers was back with a long letter that he wrote that offered excuses for himself and accused Chief Musham of dereliction of duty. He claimed that Musham had been to the theater on October 23 and inspected it. Even though all the fire apparatus was missing at the time, he didn't feel that he could point out the problems because it wasn't his place. He said he knew he would be told that Musham had nothing to do with the theater, and Sallers needed to report the problem to management. But, Sallers said, "I was afraid to report to the management for fear that I would be discharged for being too active."

More damning evidence came to light when auditorium superintendent George Dusenberry testified that two padlocked iron gates that blocked the main stairways at the Randolph Street exit were responsible for the deaths of scores of people, primarily women, and children. The gates, he claimed, had remained locked against the frantic crowds during the terrible rush to escape, but the locks had been

One of the locked iron accordion gates, which were placed across the stairwells so that ticket holders in the "cheap seats" couldn't come downstairs and claim empty seats on the floor during the intermission. They were left locked during the fire, causing scores of deaths

"quietly removed" after the fire. Dusenberry said that it was standard practice for the management at the theater to open the gates after the intermission at the close of the second act to give people an unobstructed way of leaving the house when the show ended. He admitted that they were kept locked to stop people in the cheap seats from moving down to the more expensive seats on the floor.

Like so many others, Dusenberry stated he never received any instructions from the owners or the managers about what to do in the theater if there was a fire. Powers had told him, in a "general way," to instruct the ushers on their duties and familiarize themselves with the house. There had never been a fire drill.

When Eddie Foy was testifying, he corroborated the experience of others and said that he had never seen any fire equipment or hoses in the building. Coroner Traeger asked, "Did you consider it a dangerous lot of scenery to travel with, lights and scenery combined?"

"I don't know," Eddie replied. "I consider all scenery dangerous."

Traeger determined that Eddie had been at the theater since it had opened and was asked if there had been any drills or precautions taken in case there was an emergency, like a fire.

"No," Eddie stated firmly. "I know I couldn't smoke in the theater."

"Did you notice any fire extinguishers of any kind on the stage?"

"No, sir, I did not."

"Any appliances of any kind to be used in case of fire?"

Eddie again told him that he had not seen anything of the kind. He was questioned on this for quite some time and about the asbestos curtain that was supposed to be lowered to protect the audience from fire on the stage.

He was asked, "Mr. Foy, when you came out to the footlights to try and quiet the people and you cried for the curtain to come down, did you see the curtain come down?"

"I did not see the curtain come down," Eddie stated. "I screamed for the curtain to come down, and I told the orchestra to keep up the music, and then I addressed the audience, thinking that I would get the curtain down. I would have been in front of the curtain as it came down."

"When you counseled the audience to keep quiet were you working on the assumption that there was a fire brigade on the stage?" the jury asked him.

Eddie shrugged a little. "Well, my idea was to get the curtain down and stop the panic. The audience was composed of women and children."

The inquest was supposed to only last six days, but it went on through the month of January as court stenographers compiled hundreds of pages of witness testimony. Witness after witness told of trying - and often failing - to force open exists from both inside and outside the theater. They also told of remarkable escapes and gruesome deaths - all of it in graphic detail.

James Strong, the Chicago man who escaped through a transom and tried to force open a locked door, told the jury about his experience. His wife, mother, and niece had all perished in the fire.

A.W. Menard testified that he went to a lower fire escape exit in the balcony and tried to get out that way. "It was hidden by a drape," he said, "and many people passed it not knowing it was an exit. When I attempted to open it, I could not, so I went to a second exit. That, too, was covered by drapery, but I got it open and took my family out that way."

Mrs. Josephine Petry had a seat in the upper balcony but could not sit down at first because the seats were filled, and people were standing four deep behind them. She recalled when the fire began and how several people quickly got up, only to be told to "keep your seats; there is nothing the matter." Josephine fled the theater, and even when she ran into about 100 patrons jamming the stairs to escape, she slipped past them and made it out. "When I left," she told the jury, "the charred remnants of the scenery were falling down in large chunks on the stage, and the lights were so bright they scared me."

Mrs. James Pinedo arrived late for the show and managed to get a standing-room-only ticket. She described the start of the fire and Eddie Foy's appearance, asking everyone to stay calm. She said that everyone - the audience, mostly women and children - remained quiet and calm for at least two minutes, but when a big ball of flame shot out from the stage, she realized it was time to get out. "I walked quietly to what I thought was an exit," she recalled, "and there was a little man there before me who had torn aside the drapery, and I saw an iron door or doors heavily bolted, and we couldn't get them open."

The man asked an usher to open the door, but the usher refused. He only watched at first as they struggled with the complicated locking system and finally agreed to help. Of course, he couldn't open it either since he hadn't been trained how to do so. In the end, it didn't matter. Mrs. Pinedo described a powerful wind from the stage that hit them from behind. "Those iron doors blew open, and blew us into the alley," she said. "That was my last recollection. I was then safe."

Ella Churcher was sitting in the fourth row from the back wall of the theater in the balcony. When the fire began, she and her friends fled toward an exit. "As we turned for one last look, I caught a tongue of fire leaping to the gallery and a cloud of smoke with it," she told the jury. "We got heat from it, scorching and blistering both of my ear and both my nostrils and scorching my hair. At that instant, we stepped out on the marble stairway, right out of it, and we got down the stairs safely, and then we passed out to the street."

Dr. Lester Sackett attended the show that afternoon with his wife, daughter, and sister-in-law. They were seated in the third row of the balcony and had a clear view of the stage when the fire began., "We could see sparks dropping," he recalled. "We could not see the light itself, but could see those sparks." A ripple of fear went through those seated around

Dr. Lester Sackett

the family as it became apparent that something was seriously wrong.

"There was much excitement in the vicinity of my seats," said Dr. Sackett, "with no gentlemen nearer than the three gentlemen sitting a little further to my right and back in the second section from us toward the rear were two young men - all others were women and children."

The doctor rose to his feet and tried to keep everyone around him calm. There was more danger from panic, he believed, than from the fire. "I never dreamed the fire could reach us there," he admitted. "We had to keep our position in the seats. As I had counseled others to keep quiet, and it would not look very well for us to take the lead and run, we remained there until my wife said to me, 'Everyone has left their seats, and we must get out of here.'"

Dr. Sackett looked down at the stage, saw the flames that were now leaping up into the scenery, and nodded to his wife. "It is a race with death," he said to her. He grabbed his daughter, wife, and sister-in-law and crowded them into the aisle, joining the horde attempting to escape the building.

But they were pushed back into the row of seats.

Realizing they would die if he didn't do something, he snatched up his little girl. He directed his wife and her sister to start climbing over the tops of the seats, crossing the balcony at an angle, and hurrying toward a light that he could see coming from an open door.

"I didn't look back after I started," he told the jury.

The family scrambled over the seats and made it to the door. Luckily, it was one of the doors that had a fire escape attached to it. When they got there, the door was standing open, and Dr. Sackett testified that they would not have survived if it had not been open. It was no sooner than they started through it when the huge fireball from the stages whooshed out into the auditorium. Dr. Sackett's ears and nose were badly burned, as was his sister-in-law's face.

As they rushed down the stairs, they ran into two women running *up* the fire escape. They were scared and badly confused, and even when the doctor told them to turn around and go down, they kept coming up the stairs. He eventually had to take hold of one of the women and physically turn her around so that he could save her life.

The Chicago schoolgirl named Ruth Michel, who was sitting in the second row of the gallery with three friends and had a man tell her that if she got out of her seat that he'd "knock out heads off," also testified for the coroner.

Ruth recounted the falling of the asbestos curtain and how it got stuck on the way down. It caught fire, she said, before it even reached the stage, and then a strong wind came out beneath it and blew the flames out into the audience.

At that point, Ruth and her friends weren't scared of a man who threatened to knock their heads off - they had to run. "We got out of our seats," she said, "go out of an exit all right and went out on the fire escape. I got down two of three steps and we were driven back by the flames below us. The heat came up just like a furnace and I went up two or three steps and then I got under a railing and dropped to the alley. I lit on my toes and a man caught me at the same time, so I wasn't hurt. The distance was the same as from the fourth-floor window of the building across the alley. Men in the alley called to me not to jump, but I knew I had to jump or else burn up. The flames were coming right behind me."

Ruth wiped away a tear as she recalled for Coroner Traeger how close she had come to death. Even the veteran coroner was moved by her story.

"I am only surprised that you escaped alive to tell of it," he said to her softly.

As this dramatic testimony continued in the city council chamber, politics as usual were continuing in the rest of City Hall. Theater owners and managers - angry over Mayor Harrison's belated crackdown on code violations - were lobbying Chicago aldermen for help. At first, the managers and owners agreed among themselves to make all improvements and repairs and to comply with everything the mayor wanted. But as days passed and well over 100 dance halls, meeting rooms, and even churches were closed by the city building department, the spirit of cooperation quickly faded. The theater owners began meeting with a special committee of aldermen who had been appointed to examine the new ordinances, which would not only be expensive to execute but would keep the theaters closed and thousands of people out of work indefinitely.

By January 20, newspapers across the city were reporting that the city council would reconsider and revise the new theater ordinances because the general feeling along the aldermen was that "the essentials demanded of theaters were too stringent."

Even in those days, politicians knew that if they waited long enough after a tragedy, public anger would start to fade, and little more than "thoughts and prayers" would be implemented to prevent the same things from happening the next time.

Meanwhile, the inquest continued, and on January 22, Iroquois co-owners and managers Harry Powers and Will Davis appeared separately before the jury. Neither of them was allowed to be present during the other man's testimony.

Powers was a heavy, balding man who spotted a large handlebar mustache. He, of course, placed the responsibility for the management of the theater squarely on Will Davis. He was the "active manager," Powers explained, while he, Powers, was the passive official in conducting the Iroquois' affairs. The theater had no fire equipment because Sallers, the house fireman responsible for that, had not been ordered. Deputy Fire Marshal Campion had recommended Sallers for the job, and it had been Davis who hired him. So, it was all his fault, Powers assured the jury.

As a stockholder, director, and treasurer of the Iroquois Theater Company, Powers said he was associated with it "only in a general way." He was a layman, he said, and just an interested party. Besides, Klaw and Erlanger were also interested stockholders, and they had also approved the plans.

Iroquois Theater co-owner Harry Powers, who did all he could to shift blame from himself to his partner

About the only thing that Powers admitted to was that he knew the law required signs over the exits, and although the theater had been open for five weeks, he really had no idea that the signs were not in place.

"While I acted as an assistant manager," he said, "it was in more of an advisory capacity or in consultation. All orders were given through Mr. Davis."

Unaware that he had been blamed for everything by his partner, Will Davis took the stand next. He was a slender, soft-spoken man with thinning gray hair. He sat rigidly in the witness chair.

During his questioning, Davis refused to blame anyone, saying that he had confidence in the theater's employees and believed that the Fuller Company would construct the building in compliance with all local ordinances. It was true that he had been managing theaters in Chicago for two decades but only had a general knowledge of ordinances and building. That was not the side of the business that he usually dealt with.

The Iroquois' second owner, Will Davis

He was asked about the exit signs and, like Powers, replied that he didn't know they were not in place. He also said that he didn't know the theater was lacking fire equipment. When asked whose duty it was to see to those things, he answered, "Well, I don't know that I could say. We had a fireman there sent by the city fire department." Davis said that he considered it the house fireman's duty to issue requisitions for what was needed. When none were given to him, he assumed that nothing was required.

Coroner Traeger was skeptical. "Do you want to give us the idea that you placed all the responsibility as to the fire apparatus upon the fireman, Mr. Sallers?"

Davis frowned. "I do not want to place the responsibility on anybody."

But Traeger pressed him. "As president of the company, do you want to assume the responsibility yourself?"

"I do not."

"Do you not think that as general manager it was your duty to see that those fire appliances were there to protect the public?"

"I had employees there in whom I had every confidence."

"You say you left the matter of fire protection to your employees. To which ones did you leave it?"

"Oh, I couldn't say to anyone in particular."

Of course, he couldn't.

But that would not be what newspaper reporters would consider the "bombshell" to come out of the inquest. That happened just before the conclusion of the hearing when Davis spoke of talking with Building Commissioner George Williams after Williams had inspected the theater.

And what was the result of that inspection? Davis was asked, and he stated that Williams told him that the Iroquois was "the safest and most complete theater he had ever seen."

That was an issue since Williams had testified that Inspector Edward Loughlin had inspected the theater and that he had accepted his findings because he "supposed the whole building was completed. I did not know the theater was violating any ordinances until after the fire. I was not familiar with these ordinances. I have been head of the department for only a few months and have not had the time to get things in shape."

Loughlin had testified that he had inspected the building only. The inspection of fire equipment was not his responsibility - someone from the fire department should have done that.

There had also been a second - or was it the third if Davis was telling the truth about Williams? - inspector in the building before it opened, Julian Lense. He claimed that he only went out of curiosity, though, not for an "official" inspection. He admitted that the building was not complete, but it was basically not his problem since he wasn't there in an official capacity.

So, who was lying? Was someone paid off? Did someone speak out of turn about who was in the building? And why would these city officials consider the theater safe? Even if they were not supposed to be looking for fire equipment, it was apparent that the construction company had not completed the work - not when it opened and not five weeks later when disaster struck.

The Iroquois Theater had been a ticking time bomb that finally went off - and took the lives of hundreds of people with it when it went.

13. GRAND JURY

The deliberations of the jury in the Coroner's Inquest took only days. On January 25, it was announced that a verdict had been returned. It was recommended that Mayor Harrison, Fire Marshal Musham, Will Davis, Building Commissioner Williams, Inspector Loughlin, house fireman Sallers, stage carpenter James Cummings, and light operator William McMullen all be held for action by the grand jury.

City ordinances had been violated - on fire alarm and firefighting equipment, on the regulation of dampers and flues on and above the stage, and on the fireproofing of scenery and woodwork. Aisles were enclosed on both sides of the lower boxes, and there was no fire apparatus on the orchestra floor or in the balcony or gallery.

The asbestos curtain was, of course, found to be a fraud.

Davis was held responsible for not following the law. As president and general manager, he was obligated to see that his employees were properly instructed about what to do in case of fire.

Mayor Harrison was held responsible for having "shown a lamentable lack of force, and for his efforts to escape responsibility, evidenced by the testimony of Musham and Williams; and as heads of departments under the mayor, following this weak course has given Chicago inefficient service which makes such calamity as the Iroquois Theater horror a menace until the public service is purged of incompetents."

They found Commissioner Williams guilty of "gross neglect of his duty in allowing the theater to open when the theater was incomplete and did not comply with building ordinances."

Fire Marshal Musham was responsible for "gross neglect of duty in not enforcing the city ordinances and failure to have his subordinate, William Sallers, report to him the lack of fire apparatus in the theater."

Sallers wasn't "going to be lynched," but he was accused of failing to report the lack of fire equipment. McMullen had been careless handling the light, and Cummins was charged with failing to provide the stage with proper lighting protection.

Each man posted bail and was released. Musham and Davis refused to speak to anyone, including reporters, but Mayor Harrison was said to be "furious," and Commissioner Williams was "downcast." Williams had good reason to be depressed - 11 days later, some of his inspectors were caught taking bribes from building contractors. I mean, it was the "Chicago way," but it would have been a good idea to at least wait until the ashes of the Iroquois had cooled off, so to speak.

When he finally spoke to reporters, the mayor said that the jury's findings were political and based on "flimsy charges." He added that the jury members had been hand-picked by a political enemy, Deputy Coroner Lawrence Buckley, to make him look bad.

The mayor was eventually cleared, and the press speculated that he owed his freedom to the fact that City Hall department heads testified that prior to the theater's opening, Harrison had issued a blanket order to the License Department that no theater licenses should be issued except after the approval of Commissioner Williams. That testimony, while clearing the mayor, made it so that indicting Williams for malfeasance was unavoidable.

Although officially off the hook, Harrison was deeply wounded by the scores of scathing editorials and articles that were written about him. Nearly every newspaper in Chicago spoke out against him, as did the *New York Times, Detroit Journal, Kansas City Star*, and dozens of others. It was the overwhelming opinion that the Iroquois had been a "hopeless death trap." While Harrison might not be legally responsible for what happened in the theater, he helped foster the climate that allowed the loss of life there to occur.

The John B. McCutcheon cartoon of "His Sunday Dinner" that appeared in the *Tribune*

The front page of the *Chicago Tribune* became a sore spot for the embattled mayor. He was lampooned in a series of cartoons by John T. McCutcheon, who would later become the paper's first Pulitzer Prize winner. The cartoons included Chicago cops boarding up the theater entrance while

Harrison, Musham, and Williams tried to get out the blocked exit door without success.

But the McCutcheon cartoon that moved Chicagoans the most was one the artist captioned "His Sunday Dinner." It showed a hollow-eyed, grief-stricken sitting in front of an untouched meal with his infant son, his only companion at a table surrounded by empty chairs and a high stool. In the window was a Christmas wreath, and behind him, on the wall, a framed plaque featured an inscription that read, "Blessed are the Poor in Spirit."

On the front page of the *Record-Herald*, artist Ralph Wilder published a cartoon that captured both sadness and anger. In a schoolroom filled with children, one sad child, with his chin in his hand, looks not at his schoolbook but across the aisle at an empty desk and chair. It was captioned "The Vacant Seat."

There were many broken people in Chicago in the winter of 1903-1904. Some were saddened by the maudlin cartoons and lengthy articles that blamed city officials, but others were simply shattered by the tragedy - and went to extraordinary lengths to try and cope.

One such person was Arthur Hull, the husband and father who lost his family in the disaster and pushed the hardest for arrest warrants in the wake of the fire. He became a crusader on behalf of fire victims, co-founded the Iroquois

Memorial Association - and was driven to extremes by his grief.

On the heels of the arrest warrants, Hull had filed a manslaughter suit against everyone who had been charged, but through his attorney, Thomas D. Knight, he dropped the suit a week later, saying that he was satisfied with the coroner's inquest and the subsequent grand jury proceedings. That satisfaction only lasted about two weeks, though, ending when the coroner's jury findings against Mayor Harrison were overturned by a writ of habeas corpus, and the prosecutor and judge expressed the public opinion that charges against the mayor were unlikely to be prosecuted.

Arthur Hull

By then, Hull was collaborating with the *Chicago Inter-Ocean*; the Republican newspaper determined to blame the Democratic mayor for everything connected to the theater tragedy. For his part, Hull was content to punish the mayor, but he always wanted to empty the pockets of the Iroquois owners and *Mr. Bluebeard* producers Klaw and Erlanger. With the *Inter Ocean* fanning his fury, Hull launched a public campaign against everyone involved and everyone he felt wasn't as determined to bring officials down as he was. He started with two of the grand jury members, alleging a conflict of interest. The two men, Phillip Sharkey and Ernst Heldmaier, had contracts with the city, and Heldmaier was a subcontractor who sometimes laid stonework for the Fuller Construction Company. When the prosecutor and other attorneys made it clear that the two men would not be removed from the grand jury, Hull began to insist that there had been a gas explosion during the Iroquois fire as a result of flammable chemicals brought to the theater by the company of *Mr. Bluebeard*.

He was desperate - and perhaps a bit unhinged.

On January 18, 1904, he made a startling announcement - 2,000 physicians were willing to donate money for a large hospital on the site of the Iroquois Theater if the lease on the property was ended. The owners then had to agree to sell it to the Iroquois Memorial Association - founded and created by Hull - for the purpose of erecting the hospital. It never happened, and the "2,000 doctors" never came forward with the funds.

Next, Hull persuaded several Chicago business people to join him in hiring independent investigators to collect evidence about the fire, an attorney to sift through it, and another attorney to then submit that to a second grand jury. But instead of waiting for the evidence to be compiled - or maybe because it wasn't forthcoming, or perhaps because the businessmen weren't impressed with what was found - Hull began claiming that a conspiracy to hide the truth was occurring. He soon produced a flyer that claimed, "powerful influences are at work to prevent the punishment of those responsible."

At the same time, the *Inter-Ocean* was continuing the blathering about Chicago's evil mayor and the crooked grand jury proceedings, which likely led to Hull believing that he had strong support in the press. In truth, though, the silence about Hull's accusations in the city's other newspapers, especially the *Tribune*, should have told him that he was going down the wrong path. But it didn't, and finally, Hull announced that he was giving up all his business activities to focus on nothing but punishing those responsible for the fire.

This went on until February 13, 1904, when the grand jury demanded Hull present his proof. He was subpoenaed to explain and substantiate his accusations, and during a closed-door meeting between Hull and the state's attorney, he was questioned by the jurors. He was finally forced to admit that he had no evidence of bias, an explosion, or of any kind of conspiracy.

The broken man's crusade was finally over.

A short time later, Hull resigned from the Iroquois Memorial Association and announced that he was headed first to Kansas City, then California, and might never return to Chicago.

But a year later, he did return, and he married Emma Louise Firmenich, daughter of wealthy starch producer and homeopathic physician, Dr. Joseph Firmenich. Though he described himself as an attorney at this point in his life, he served as the president of the J.P. Wood Claim and Adjustment Company and made a large amount of money.

His months away from Chicago had apparently helped to ease his grief, and he went on to lead a full and rather exciting life, serving in the U.S. Navy, motoring through Yosemite, befriending famous magician Harry Kellar, founding the town of Niland, California, and working as a realtor in Los Angeles in the 1920s.

He passed away in 1944.

Arthur Hull, as troubling as his actions were, was motivated by his deep sense of profound grief at the loss of his family. He was not one of the many who immediately tried to cash in on the tragedy.

According to a review, one songwriter composed something called "The Burning of the Iroquois Theater" that "droned on for four pages and two verses." Another turn, "The Iroquois on Fire," appeared and then disappeared almost as quickly as it had arrived - mercifully.

A writer, Wesley S. Stranger, turned out a fictional potboiler called *Rescued from a Fiery Death* that sold poorly. A more substantial book, filled with first-person accounts, called *The Great Chicago Theater Disaster*, was written by

Marshall Everett later in 1904 and sold quite well. For many years, it was the only chronicle of events available, and even today, it's a worthwhile contemporary collection of accounts.

Within hours of the tragedy, a Hartford insurance company inserted a large ad in a Chicago newspaper that ran next to a long list of fire victims. The ad read: "9 million dead or injured in the U.S. last year by accidents. Protect yourself by insuring with the Travelers Insurance Company."

Accurate - but unbelievably tasteless.

And they weren't alone. The Orr and Lockwood Hardware store, which had rushed over hundreds of lanterns on the day of the fire, began running ads for dry powder extinguishers with the thoughtful suggestion, "Get it Today - You May Need it Tonight."

In early January, the Klein Optical Company of Chicago bought advertising space to say, "We are receiving many inquiries concerning lantern slides and films of the Iroquois Theater Fire. There were no moving pictures or lantern slides made of the fire. Our offices were almost adjacent to the theater, but commercialism gave way before the sight of bodies piled up on the sidewalks and the horror of the catastrophe."

Or so they claimed.

The ad went on from there: "We should have ready six lantern slides. One will show the exterior, almost undamaged. The other five will be taken from drawings by artist Charles Lederer, who was present at the fire. They will show characteristic scenes, but ghastly sensationalism will be absent."

I guess commercialism won out after all.

On the same note, with even less credibility, one newspaper, the *Clipper*, advertised that the S. Lubin Company of Philadelphia had a "Film of the Chicago Theater Fire," and a week later, it ran an ad for "Asbestos Curtains from the Tiffin Scenery Company of Tiffin, Ohio."

Billboard magazine was running ads for a new road manager for *Mr. Bluebeard* while some of the cast was still in the hospital being treated for their injuries. They also advertised the Boswell Electric and Optical Company in Chicago, offering a package of 20 color slides from the fire - complete with "lecture" - for just $7.50.

Hundreds of thousands of extra newspapers sold in the wake of the fire, especially when there was big news - like the announcement of indictments by the grand jury on February 23.

In a statement, the grand jury said, "The jury believes the direct duty of protecting lives of those in the theater lay upon persons responsible for furnishing apparatus necessary to extinguish fire." This duty, jury members found, was the responsibility of Will Davis, business manager Thomas Noonan - who had been cleared by the coroner's jury - and stage carpenter James Cummings. All three were indicted for manslaughter. The charges against Musham, Sallers, and McMullen were dismissed for lack of evidence.

It was obvious to the jury - as it was to practically anyone else - that city ordinances for the proper inspection of theaters had been ignored when it came to the Iroquois. They issued indictments against Building Commissioners Williams and Loughlin for "palpable omission of duty."

The jury exonerated Mayor Harrison but took him to task for his many failures in overseeing the men in his administration who had allowed the disaster to happen. Harrison, of course, brushed the whole thing aside, claiming that his enemies were merely out to get him.

The state's prosecutor, Charles Dineen, knew he had an uphill battle ahead of him when it was time to take the cases to trial. It would be hard to prove guilt because you can't "prosecute a locked door."

Days after the fire, while at the end of a blind gallery where passage should have been, but because of a locked exit, at least 30 had died, Dineen urged Coroner Traeger to try and discover the identities of those who had perished at that spot. In order to prosecute manslaughter, Dineen had to identify one or more of the victims whose deaths were specifically caused by the locked door.

A moral responsibility was easily fixed, Dineen knew, as well as civic responsibility, but finding someone guilty in a court of law was another matter entirely. The case had already been tried in the newspapers. Now it had to be done in a courtroom, and it soon became a long and dramatic battle for the heart and soul of the city.

14. THE VERDICT

The fight for the defense in the case was led by a tough Chicago attorney named Levy Mayer. Born in Richmond, Virginia, to Jewish Bavarian immigrants, his parents were caught up in the Civil War when he was only a child and moved the family north to the Midwest, first to Milwaukee, then Chicago.

Levy's father went into the tobacco business but fared poorly. Henry Mayer was a highly educated man but had no head for the business, causing the family to live near poverty. Young Levy, a brilliant student, decided on a law career before ever finishing high school. With financial help from an older brother, he entered Tale Law School at age 16. Levy was so advanced that the minimum age requirement of 18 had been waived for him. He graduated in 1876, second in his class. Back in Chicago, he was too young to be admitted to the bar, so he took a job at the Chicago Law Institute, where he wrote for legal papers, edited books, and helped attorneys with research. This early experience paid off handsomely for him, and when he was admitted to the bar in 1877, he was described as having "a remarkable knowledge of case law."

Defense attorney Levy Mayer

Levy and his partner flourished in Chicago's Gilded Age with its rapidly changing business and industrial conditions. Though he began in criminal law, he soon gained a reputation for expertise in corporate, business, and antitrust law, working with some of the biggest companies in the city, from the Chicago Telephone Company to the Union Stock Yards.

In late 1903, Levy was 43 years old and the founding partner of his firm. He was considered one of the city's brightest and most aggressive lawyers - a "legal genius of the commercial age." He was a man who could quickly and accurately absorb all the aspects of a case, and while he remained calm in the courtroom, he was seen as a combative adversary. He was also physically imposing, with long, swept-back, dark hair and standing nearly six feet tall.

As might be expected after such a description, not everyone liked Levy Mayer. Mayor Harrison - who had once crossed sword with him during a battle over reforming the city's hiring system to award jobs based on merit rather than on political patronage - dismissed Mayer as a "political schemer" and one of "a bold, unscrupulous, crafty, powerful lot of machine politicians who would be lined up for my undoing."

Remember, *everyone* was out to get Mayor Harrison, or so he always claimed.

In less than a day after the Iroquois fire, Klaw and Erlanger, who kept insisting they had only a marginal financial interest at the Iroquois, asked Mayer to act as special counsel to represent not only their interests but those of Davis and the others who were going to be indicted by the grand jury. After an all-night session with members of the Theatrical Trust, Mayer's firm was selected to lead the defense team. It would be one of the major criminal cases of his career and certainly showed a willingness to take part in an unpopular case. Even the worst defendants were entitled to a defense.

And as far as the city was concerned, they were some of the worst. At first, Chicago had been numbed by the horror. But it became enraged as indictments were handed down, and one of the defendants, Will Davis, was reported saying, "If the people had remained in their seats and not been excited by the cry of fire, not a single life would have been lost."

While preparing for the trial, Mayer and his staff thumbed through hundreds of pages of Chicago's building and safety ordinances, studying them line by line. The determining question was whether the ordinances were valid or not. Mayer, for one, believed they were not. He took the position that the essential point was whether there was any cause and effect between the conditions of the theater and the fire. In other words, did the fire start because the theater was not up to code?

Despite the anger and grief surrounding the inquest and the grand jury indictments, Mayer had two things in his favor - time and a public distracted by other events. The fire had started to slip off the front pages within two weeks of the disaster, only briefly returned when something new developed. Plenty of other things were going on in the news at the time, including a major late-winter snowstorm that had closed the city streets for days.

Mayer searched for loopholes in the city ordinances, taking advantage of these distractions, crowded court calendars, and other legal delay tactics. He also used local prejudice against his clients, arguing in late September 1904, almost a year after the fire, that because feelings about the tragedy were still "running so high in Chicago," he wanted a change of venue to Peoria, Illinois. There he thought Noonan and Cummings could get a "fair and impartial trial." A few days later, he filed a motion to quash the manslaughter charge against Davis.

Over the objections of prosecutors, the trial was moved to Peoria for Noonan and Cummings. In early November, a Chicago and Peoria judge heard the argument to quash the Davis indictment. On February 9, 1905, Mayer scored a major victory when both judges tossed out the indictments against Davis, Noonan, and Cummings. The state's case was beginning to collapse.

Neither of the judges believed the tragedy had been caused by the failure of the three defendants to provide adequate fire apparatus. The fire had been caused by a light, which had not been placed in the theater by any of the men.

With these announcements, Mayer told the press that "any future indictments would not be worth the paper they were written on."

But state prosecutors disagreed and, less than a month later, on March 7, 1905, using evidence re-submitted by witnesses to the fire, a second Chicago grand jury again indicted Davis on manslaughter charges, along with Loughlin and Building Commissioner Williams. The jury refused to indict Klaw and Erlanger, Powers, Cummings, Sallers, and Noonan.

Once more, Mayer argued for a motion to quash the indictments and, once more, time worked in his favor. Because of overloaded dockets and other delays within the Illinois courts system, It was not until January 13, 1906, that the Davis indictment was sustained. Preparations were made for a new trial to start - and then were delayed again.

Mayer once again demanded a change of venue, and it was finally granted in June 1906. The Davis trial was moved to Danville, Illinois, a small farming community in Vermilion County, 134 miles south of Chicago. To locals, the Iroquois Theater Fire was something long ago and far away from their daily lives.

It was nearly three years after the fire, but the state refused to give up. They planned to present an overwhelming argument against Davis and the others. Assistant State's Attorneys James J. Barbour, a team of stenographers, and 22 witnesses - some of whom were relatives of the dead and others who were survivors of the fire - boarded the train to Danville on the night before the trial.

On March 7, 1907, the courtroom was packed in anticipation of a long, highly charged battle. It had been leaked in the press that the state was prepared to summon not 22 but 200 witnesses, some of them horribly disfigured from the fire. The first witness would be a Chicago housewife, Maude Jackson, whose daughter, Viva, had been one of the victims.

When Mrs. Jackson took the stand, Mayer interrupted the proceedings to introduce a motion to compel the state to immediately introduce the Chicago city ordinances on which the manslaughter indictment was based. The motion was granted.

Viva Jackson

Over the next two days, Mayer presented a 231-page brief to Judge E.R.E. Kimbrough, Vermilion County prosecutor, and John W. Keeslar. But that wasn't all he did to get attention. In a theatrical gesture, the doors to the courtroom were opened, and a procession of hotel bellhops and porters entered with stacks of law books that they heaped onto the defense table. While his associates arranged the books into stacks, Mayer continued his presentation as though nothing unusual had just happened.

Against a backdrop of Chicago city maps that defined fire limits and the locations of various theaters, Mayer argued that Chicago safety ordinances were not valid because they were legally "beyond the power of the city under the Illinois Constitution and state statutes." He explained that Chicago had only such power as was given to it by the state legislature and that no such powers had been given to the Chicago city council. He maintained there had been an unlawful delegation of power when the city gave to a separate entity - the Chicago Board of Fire Underwriters - control over sprinkler systems in buildings. That negligence could not rest on Davis' failure to supply fire equipment that was demanded in the ordinances. Simply put, he said, "a reasonable man is not required to take all possible precautions but merely those which would be taken by an ordinary prudent man under the circumstances."

It was complicated, but it made a sort of legal sense. If the city ordinances were not valid, then how could Davis be guilty of not following them?

The case ended on March 9. Mayer concluded his closing arguments by saying, "It was the hand of God that brought about the loss of lives in the fire and Will J. Davis was no more responsible for their deaths than if a hurricane had lifted the roof off the theater."

Personally, I don't buy the argument, but it doesn't matter because Judge Kimbrough did. He ruled the Chicago ordinances were invalid and inadmissible as evidence. When Prosecutor Keeslar, in a desperate late in the trial move, asked not only permission to drop the indictment against Davis but also to not to formally acquit him, Mayer objected, jumped to his feet, and demanded that Davis receive "the verdict he is entitled to." He urged the judge to reject the motion.

Because the state had insufficient proof of manslaughter without the ordinances, Judge Kimbrough directed the jury to deliver a not-guilty verdict. He said he was compelled to do so because of the law, not his personal choice.

"If it were in my power to bring back to life and put the bloom of youth into the cheeks of these young girls, two of whom I personally knew, by incarcerating the defendant in this case in the penitentiary for the term of his natural life, I believe I would do it," the judge said. "But I cannot."

As one reporter wrote, "He left no doubt that he considered Davis morally guilty, but he said his duty was to hold strictly to the letter of the law."

Davis wept as the verdict was returned. Afterward, he told reporters that he was confident that he would be acquitted because "those who died were the victims of circumstance over which I could have no control."

Three and a half years after the fire, charges against the theater official were formally dismissed. All attempts to hold anyone associated with the theater criminally liable for the tragedy came to an end.

The conduct of the case was severely criticized in the *Illinois Law Review*, which complained about the "outrageous delays caused by a lack of dispatch in the conduct of the prosecution" about Mayer's methods of "postponing motions to quash indictments and for charges of venue." In the Iroquois case, the *Review* writer said, "sows the seeds of contempt for the law and gives noticed to the world of the inefficiency of our judicial system."

And such methods may have been criticized in 1906, but they remain the standard for legal proceedings today.

While attorneys debated the ruling, with some claiming the new post-fire city ordinances had the same flaws, Will Davis returned to Chicago to be given a welcoming party by theater owners and performers.

There would be no good news for the relatives of victims seeking monetary damage from the theater. Not only was no one ever charged with a criminal act, but few of the families that tried to seek compensation were never awarded a dime. More than 275 civil lawsuits were filed, some of them within days of the fire, but nothing was paid out. To make matters worse, most of the fire victims were not covered by life insurance. Except for the wealthy, few women and children were insured in the early 1900s.

The theater had been insured by a liability policy from the Maryland Casualty Company, which had the "usual limit of $10,000 on any one accident, and $5,000 for any one life. The policy, however, provides that it does not cover loss from injuries caused by boiler explosions, the use of explosives, or by fire."

The Iroquois Theater Company filed for bankruptcy soon after the disaster.

But some of the grieving families didn't give up. In February 1905, Henry Shabad, an attorney who lost both his children in the fire, reportedly went to New York to seek evidence for an indictment of Klaw and Erlanger.

The following October, two women, relatives of fire victims, brought a $50,000 lawsuit against the Iroquois Theater Company and the Fuller Construction Company. There was no report on the outcome of these actions, but it was likely a disappointing one.

Rumors did swirl for a while that the Klaw and Erlanger organization did pay off relatives of some of the victims, but there is no evidence of that - and I'd have to add that it's unlikely to be true.

It seems that the only things that survivors of the Iroquois Theater Fire ever received were injuries, nightmares, heartbreak, and many years of grief.

15. AFTERMATH

While cold comfort to the dead and their families, it can be said that those who perished at the Iroquois did not die in vain. From the public outcry over the tragedy came strict reforms in building and fire safety codes throughout the country - not only in theaters but also in public structures like schools, churches, and office buildings.

Floor plans that clearly showed the location of exits began to be included in playbills, and for years, an announcement on playbill covers noted: "Look around now, choose the nearest exit. In case of fire, walk, do not run. Do not try and beat your neighbor to the street."

The use of fireproof materials for scenery became mandatory, with reformers stating that, as long as that risk remained, there would be panic in the audience and panic causes disaster." Concerns about mob panic were proven to be well-founded later in the century with two horrible examples of it - the 1942 Coconut Grove nightclub fire in Boston, where 491 died and hundreds were injured, and the 1944 Ringling Brothers' Circus Fire in Hartford, Connecticut, in which 168 were killed, two-thirds of them children.

Reforms also called for exit signs that were illuminated and exit doors that opened out rather than in. Schools began using these reforms to improve their safety standards, running fire drills that put emphasis on the time it took to get everyone out of the school buildings. Unfortunately, though, some cities and schools took too much time to implement changes. Five years after the Iroquois disaster, 171 children and two teachers died in a fire in Collinwood, Ohio, because of exit doors that opened in and not out. Like at the Iroquois, many of the victims were trampled in the crush.

From the Iroquois Fire came a device that is still widely used today. Carl Prinzler, a hardware salesman from Indianapolis, had tickets for the show on October 30, but work caused him to run late, and he missed it. He was so disturbed by the loss of life in the tragedy that he became determined to solve one of the main problems that had doomed the audience - the inability to open exit doors that were locked or bolted.

Prinzler and his neighbor, an architectural engineer named Henry DuPont, came up with a simple crossbar contraption that they called the "Self-Releasing Fire Exit Bolt." They marketed the bolt in 1908 through a hardware company in Indianapolis, and it caught on. Theaters were updating in the wake of the fire, and the bolt - now commonly called a "panic bar" - became a commercial success.

Benjamin Marshall, the young, relatively inexperienced architect who designed the Iroquois, was blamed by some people for his poor design of converging stairways. But Marshall designed other Chicago buildings, including the Blackstone Theater, the Drake Hotel, and the Edgewater Hotel. In a detailed oral history that he recorded many years later for an architectural resource library at the University of Texas in Austin, he discussed his career in great length.

But he never once mentioned the Iroquois Theater.

Eddie Foy returned to the New York stage in 1904 after a few months in vaudeville and took a leading role on Broadway in a musical called *Piff! Paff! Poof!* For many years, he received rounds of applause from audiences who remembered his bravery during the fire. He eventually formed an act with his children billed "The Seven Little Foys."

In the early 1950s, Bob Hope played Eddie in a film filled with dozens of errors in its representation of the Iroquois Fire.

Eddie died in 1928 in the kind of place where he'd spent most of his professional life - a hotel room. He was 72 years old.

The beautiful Annabelle Whitford, who played the part of Stella, Queen of the Fairies, eventually became one of the famed Ziegfeld Girls. She retired from the stage in 1910 when she married Dr. Edward Buchan, one of the doctors who had done rescue work after the fire.

Klaw, Erlanger, and the hated Theatrical Trust saw competition threaten their operations in the 1910s and 1920s, but everyone suffered after the 1929 stock market crash, and the Trust eventually fell apart.

Will Davis continued managing theaters until he retired in 1914. After that, he faded into obscurity.

In 1935, Carter Harrison, Jr. wrote a lengthy autobiography about his life and five consecutive terms as Chicago's mayor. He devoted only three pages to the Iroquois tragedy. He blamed the fire on aldermen dragging their feet on city fire ordinances, saying nothing about his civic responsibilities. He also claimed that "public hysteria" had led to the city council closing all the city's theaters immediately after the fire.

Harrison died in 1953 at the age of 93, after writing another autobiography that never mentioned the theater at all.

Levy Mayer's corporate law practice continued to flourish in Chicago. After his success with the Davis case, he went on to represent some of the most powerful theatrical figures of the day, including producer Charles Frohmann, Klaw, Erlanger, and Florenz Ziegfeld, creator of the *Ziegfeld Follies*. But entertainment figures were only part of his expanding practice, which continues today as Mayer, Brown, Rowe, and Maw, employing hundreds of attorneys in the U.S. and overseas.

Fire Marshal Musham, his reputation badly tarnished after the coroner's inquest, quietly resigned in 1904. He died soon afterward. His white helmet remains on permanent display at the Chicago Historical Society, which also owns the spotlight that started the fire backstage.

On the day after the fire, Fireman First Class Michael Corrigan of Engine 13 was promoted for heroism to acting lieutenant. He eventually became Chicago Fire

Commissioner. No Chicago firefighter was killed in the line of duty during his tenure, which lasted from 1937 to 1955.

Charlotte Plamondon, the young woman who leaped over a railing and successfully escaped the theater with her "box party," was so shaken by her experience that she could not return to school for months.

Unfortunately, she would soon suffer another tragedy when her parents were among those lost at sea in the sinking of the *Lusitania*, torpedoed by a German submarine in 1915.

As in most American cities in the early 1900s, Chicago's many morning and evening newspapers slowly disappeared. The colorful City Press Association split into two parts in 1910 - the Press Association and the new City News Bureau - but both agencies are now defunct.

Many of the city's old school reporters also began to fade away, especially after the violent era of Prohibition.

Charles Collins, the young reporter at the Iroquois on opening night and was on the scene during the fire, would eventually end a 60-year career at the *Chicago Tribune*. He worked for many other papers along the way, once earning the distinction of being banned from all Shubert theaters because of negative reviews he'd written.

He would sometimes be called upon to write Iroquois pieces on the anniversary of the fire. Two years before his death in 1964, he said that he would never forget the sight of one victim - a beautiful blond young woman, lying nude on a marble-topped table in Thompson's Restaurant, "looking like a classic Greek statue carved in alabaster."

Around 1910, the Iroquois Memorial Hospital was built in downtown Chicago. It was converted into a tuberculosis sanatorium around 1935 and closed after World War II. It was then demolished. In the hospital, there had been a six-foot-high memorial to the Iroquois victims. It was a bronze relief designed by Laredo Taft. It disappeared when the hospital was torn down and was discovered again many years later in the basement of the City-County building. It is now on display inside the LaSalle Street entrance to City Hall, but for years, there was no explanation for it, so visitors might

The Iroquois Memorial Hospital was built in 1910 and closed after World War II

understand what it was. A plaque has since been added by the Union League Club of Chicago.

A plan to erect any other kind of memorial to the victims has never materialized. Instead, a triangular marker was placed in Montrose Cemetery by a private citizen. An even smaller plaque was affixed to the wall of an office building near the theater. That building has since been demolished, and the plaque has vanished.

The Iroquois Memorial marker that was placed in Montrose Cemetery

In 2003, the one-hundredth anniversary of the fire, another memorial plaque was unveiled by politicians and city leaders, but it was never installed at the theater, in Couch Place, or anywhere else.

For many decades after the fire, survivors would gather every December 30 at City Hall to remember the victims. Former Fire Commissioner Corrigan always attended when he was alive and brought along the alarm box that he pulled on that day. These commemorative events ended in the 1960s as the number of survivors dwindled.

The last survivor of the fire died in 1978. Harriet Gray Crumpacker was then 86 years old, and in 1903, the little Michigan City, Indiana girl had crawled beneath the legs of

The Iroquois was transformed into a vaudeville house and then re-named the Colonial Theater until it closed in 1924

Engine 13's horses after escaping from the theater by jumping into her father's arms. She said for many years after the fire, she didn't go to the theater without looking carefully at the curtains on both sides of the stage, always watching for sparks.

The Iroquois Theater itself survived the fire.
Its interior was repaired, remodeled, and updated to meet the new fire codes and reopened in 1904 as a vaudeville house called Hyde and Behmann's Music Hall. A year later, it was

renamed the Colonial Theatre. During its time in operation, a building next door caught on fire, frightening the audience.

The Colonial was shuttered on May 17, 1924, and the original building was razed nine days later to make way for the United Masonic Temple Building. The 21-story office building contained its own theater, the Oriental, a combination of vaudeville and movie house that used portions of the Iroquois - including the front façade - in its construction.

The Oriental opened in 1926 and was operated by the Balaban and Katz theater chain, then a division of Paramount Pictures. The theater thrived until the 1960s when the inner city saw a period of decline. By the 1970s, the Oriental, now in a state of disrepair, was reduced to showing low budget and exploitation films. In 1980, following a

Randolph Street and the Oriental Theater in 1958

The James M. Nederlander Theater – formerly the Oriental and Ford Center for the Performing Arts – stands on the site of the Iroquois Theater today. Many years have passed but remnants of the original theater remain

shooting at the front of the theater and the subsequent arrest of gang members inside, the Oriental closed in 1981.

It opened again a little later as the home to a wholesale electronics dealer, but it didn't last and soon went dark again.

In 1996, the Canadian theatre production company Livent bought the property and began to restore the theater with assistance from the city of Chicago. After the motor company acquired the naming rights, it reopened as the Ford Center for the Performing Arts in 1998.

When Livent declared bankruptcy a month after the theater opened, it was purchased by SFX Entertainment, which was sold to Clear Channel Communications, which later became a part of Live Nation. Finally, in 2007, it was acquired by its current owner, which operates it as the James M. Nederlander Theatre.

Oddities and mysteries about the fire linger today. It seems that official Chicago police and fire department records on the disaster do not exist. The Chicago Historical Society does not possess any records, either. According to the Cook County Courts, the records of the legal proceedings that followed the disaster were thrown out decades ago to make room for new documents.

The building next to the Iroquois in 1903 still stands at Randolph and State streets, looking just as it did back in 1903, except there is a McDonald's where a cigar store was once located. The Delaware Building, as it is known, was refurbished a few years ago and has a small lobby with a collection of framed photos of some of the prominent hotels and theaters in the vicinity. However, there is no photograph of the Iroquois and no mention of the horrible events that occurred. Instead, a later photograph of the theater building after it was refurbished, renamed, and turned into a vaudeville house.

A lot of mystery and confusion remains about the fire and is partly due to the speed with which city newspapers were forced to meet their deadlines at the time. For instance, on the day after the fire, the *Tribune* reported that doctors had revived a woman at Thompson's Restaurant, but in the same edition, a woman with the same name is listed among the dead.

The exact number of victims will never be known. The counts were all over the place - the coroner's office said 571; the *Tribune*, 575; and the *Daily News*, 475. Commissioner Corrigan stated the number as 601. The *Encyclopedia Americana* listed the deaths at 539., The National Fire Protection Association and the *World Almanac* both put the count at 602. Some of the numbers came from the fact that the death toll went up in the days after the fire as more succumbed to their injuries, and more bodies were found, but confusion remains.

Questions about the fate of many of the victims also add to the confusion.

For instance, what happened to Floraline - or "Florine" - the German aerialist who allegedly fell to the stage during the disaster?

After the fire started, the Grigolatis aerial act had little time to react. One account states Floraline was some distance away from the others and was caught in the flames by a burning piece of scenery. She panicked, lost her grip, and fell onto the stage behind the burning castle garden set below. They saw her there, unmoving, and by the time her companions were able to unhook themselves from their

The Grigolatis aerial performers – was one of these women the mysterious "Floraline?"

harnesses and get down the ladders to the stage, Floraline was gone. They could only hope that someone had carried her out to safety.

But there is still a lot of controversy about whether this story is true if Floraline or Florine was a man or a woman, and whether he or she was an actual person. Most likely, she was a woman because the Grigolatis has been described as an all-female troupe. But many believe the story of the German aerialist became confused with the story of Nellie Reed and that Floraline never existed at all.

Strangely, though, "Florine" was mentioned in the Chicago Tribune on December 31 in a story that revealed a partial list of the dead. In that story, it states that Florine died in an ambulance on the way to the hospital.

> FLORINE, a German aerial performer, taken to Samaritan Hospital, died in ambulance.

ONE AFTERNOON AT THE IROQUOIS | 283

Even the fate of Nellie Reed remains in question. Her body was taken to New York, where she was supposed to be buried, but Green-Wood Cemetery in Brooklyn has no record of her burial. British newspapers say she was being returned to London for burial but never reported whether her remains were returned home.

The controversy over the fire may have faded away many years ago, but the lessons learned from it should never be forgotten. The Iroquois Theater Fire ranks as the nation's fourth-deadliest blaze and the deadliest single theater fire in American history.

It remains one of Chicago's worst tragedies and - as you'll soon see - a perfect example of how the past continues to reverberate into the present in ways that are beyond the limits of most imaginations.

16. HAUNTED

The Iroquois Theater is long gone.

The people who worked and died here? Not so much.

After the fire, the majestic theater was remodeled, became a music hall, and then a movie theater in the 1920s. All that remains of the original building today is a single, basement-level foundation wall. Still, sightings of ghosts began almost immediately after the fire and continue today in the theater that stands in the Iroquois' place.

Employees at the most recent incarnations of the building are not supposed to talk about the ghosts. In fact, they're not even supposed to talk about the fire unless someone specifically asks them about it. But some of them do, usually outside of work or in the Couch Place alley that runs behind the building, a place where smoking breaks often occur.

According to these anonymous staff members, strange things happen here. A few have told me that curtains tend to get stuck about 10 feet above the stage - just as the fire curtain did on that fateful afternoon. Others claim that one spotlight - the one near the location of the light that started the fire - tends to break off from the now-computerized circuits and behave as though it has a mind of its own.

One day in 2004, during rehearsals for the show *Wicked*, all the doors in the building suddenly flew open. An electronic command was designed to *close* all the doors but not open them.

Many employees claim to have seen people in the balcony, particularly during rehearsals, and found no one there - and the doors locked - when they go to ask them to leave. They've seen figures in other parts of the theater, too. They are often described as shadows, flitting about the auditorium when no one living is present.

Staff members claim they have occasionally heard screams in the middle of the night and have encountered the spirit of a little girl who has been heard giggling, followed by the flushing of a backstage toilet.

Still, others have reported backstage encounters with the ghost of a woman wearing a tutu. Traditionally, this has been attributed to Nellie Reed, the aerialist who was killed in the fire. However, details of Reed's death are sketchy - the *Chicago Tribune* alone has reported several different stories, some claiming that she was stuck on a high platform and unable to get down during the fire. Others said she was in a high dressing room and afraid of elevators took the burning staircase instead. Still, other reports claim that she didn't die in the theatre but in the hospital shortly afterward.

Nellie did die after being burned at the theater but based on how confusing her story is - can we be sure that it's her ghost?

Maybe it's the ghost of the elusive Floraline? No one has ever found any information about her, other than newspaper appearances that claim she died in the ambulance on the way to the hospital.

We can assume that it must be one of these two performers, wearing a skimpy aerialist outfit when seen, because no one else in their right mind would have been wearing that kind of clothing during a Chicago winter.

But the woman in the aerial ballet costume is not the only specter seen around the theatre. Several employees have reported an apparition of a man in a red shoulder cape, and others have reported a ghost in the balcony ventilation system. The man in the cape's identity would be anyone's guess - there were, however, over 1,000 costumes used in *Mr. Bluebeard*, and the idea that one might have been wearing a red shoulder cape is undoubtedly possible. The phantoms could also be ghosts of the other employees killed. One other actor, a bit-part player named Burr Scott, died in the disaster, along with an usher and two female attendants.

Actress Ana Gasteyer, who starred in *Wicked's* long run at the theater in the 2000s, reported that she had encountered the ghost of a woman and her two small children in the theater, dressed in clothing from the early twentieth century.

After the fire, many of the victims were taken to the temporary hospital set up at Thompson's Restaurant next door or to temporary morgues at nearby C.H. Jordan's Saloon and at Marshall Field's department store, which was on the corner.

Marshall Field's, of course, still stands, although it's Macy's today. During the fire, the eighth floor -- where they sold linens, sheets, and towels - was turned into a temporary morgue for the victims.

Since that time, this floor has gained a reputation for being haunted. Many shoppers feel sadness and depression on this floor, and it's also been the site of at least two suicide attempts over the years.

Couch Place – the infamous "Death Alley" – as it looks today

There have also been reports of figures seen on this floor after closing time, but when they are approached to ask them to leave - they're gone.

But most of the hauntings connected to the Iroquois Theater Fire are found in the immediate vicinity of the building. The fire, not surprisingly, is likely the primary source of the restless spirits, but it may not account for all of them. The theaters that have occupied the spot since 1904 have their share of horror stories, too.

In addition to the shooting at the Oriental in 1980, another death occurred four decades earlier. In 1943, a patron attending a movie at the Oriental put a note to his wife, mentioning the song "You'll Never Know How Much I Miss You," a song from the movie, in his pocket. As the song played in the film, he shot himself to death.

There also have been at least two suicides behind the theater where people jumped from high buildings to their doom in the alley.

It can't come as a surprise to know that "Death Alley" is a very haunted place - often said to be more haunted than the theater itself.

Cold spots - localized areas that are about 10 degrees cooler than they ought to be - are common in haunted sites, and some say that the whole of Death Alley can sometimes be one of these "cold spots."

One witness reported hearing a strange clicking noise while entering the alley from the Dearborn Street end. This was several years ago before the alley had been cleaned up and repaved and when some of the original bricks were still visible - bricks that had seen the stain of the blood of those who had hurled themselves off the unfinished fire escapes above. As she started to walk down the alleyway, she looked for the source of the sound, only to see small rocks literally flying across the alley from one side to the other and tapping against the opposite wall with enough force to make the noise she was hearing.

Needless to say, she picked up her pace through the alley and chose another path the next time she walked in that area of downtown.

Along the theater building's back wall, where the boards had been extended from the university building to help those trapped in the alley, people in the alley have encountered eerie sensations of being touched. It was here where the bodies fell to the pavement, and more than 125 lives came to an end.

Photographs taken in the alley often appear inexplicably blurred or have mysterious lights and objects in them that cannot be seen with the naked eye. The batteries of cameras and other devices mysteriously drain, only to start working again somewhere else. Recordings that have been made here sometimes capture voices, cries, and laughter - none of which was heard by those attempting the recording. They are only heard later when it's played back.

Many who pass through Couch Place often find themselves very uncomfortable and unsettled there. They say that faint cries are sometimes heard in the shadows, and some have reported being touched by unseen hands, had their hair tugged on, or they have heard whispers so close to their ears that it causes them to jump in fright. There is never anyone close to them when it occurs - no one who is alive anyway.

Women, especially mothers, seem to have more experiences in Death Alley than anyone else. I have spoken to many who have told me they have been touched as they walk through the alley, but often it happens in a very particular way. These women often experience something that feels like a small hand holding onto their own as they walk along - as if one of the many children who died in the fire is looking for someone to take care of them.

Others say they have also heard little voices singing, shouting, and, perhaps most eerie of all, a group of children laughing and playing.

One of the most vivid experiences like this that I can recall was passed on to me one night during a Weird Chicago Tour. I had a group of people with me in Death Alley, and after explaining the history, I allowed people to walk around for a short time. During this lull in the action, a woman approached and told me about a recent night attending a play at the Nederlander Theater. She called over an usher and asked him to go out and quiet down the group of children that were being noisy outside of the theater's exit doors --- doors that led directly out into Death Alley.

She saw the same usher again later and asked him what had been going on. He shook his head, she told me, and he explained that the alley had been empty. There had been no children playing there. She apologized and said to him that she was sure what she'd heard, but the man merely shrugged.

A few nights later, she was on the Weird Chicago Tour and heard the story of what had happened in the Iroquois

Theater. She swore that she did not know the 1903 fire and had no idea before the tour that night that the alley was said to be haunted.

As ghostlore has long made clear, places where terrible, violent, and deadly events occur are often the first places to become haunted - both by the spirits of yesterday and the residual remnants of history.

The Iroquois Theater - and Death Alley - would certainly fit the bill. I have long believed that the ghosts of the past still linger here. They are stark reminders of the trauma and terror experienced by the unlucky patrons who had tickets to an afternoon matinee that day - and a chilling remembrance of a tragedy that should never be forgotten.

BIBLIOGRAPHY

Asbury, Herbert - *Gem of the Prairie*, New York, NY, Alfred Knopf, 1940

Bergreen Lawrence - *As Thousands Cheer*, New York, NY, Viking, 1990

Blum, Daniel - *A Pictorial History of the American Theater 1860-1960*, Philadelphia, PA, Chilton Book Division, 1960

Brandt, Nat - *Chicago Death Trap*, Carbondale, IL, Southern Illinois University Press, 2003

Campbell, Ballard C. - *American Disasters*, New York, NY, Checkmark Books, 2008

Chernow, Ron - *Titan*, New York, NY, Random House, 1998

Collins, Charles - "The Tragedy Chicago Will Never Forget," *Chicago Tribune*, December 28, 1952

Cramer, Kali Joy - *Sinister Chicago*, Guiford, CT, Globe-Pequot Press, 2020

Csida, Joseph and J.B. Csida - *American Entertainment*, New York, NY, Watson-Guptil Publishers, 1978

Daniel, Clifton and John Kirshon - *America's Century*, New York, NY, Dorling Kindersley, 2000

Dedmon, Emmett - *Fabulous Chicago*, New York, NY, Atheneum Books, 1981

Ditzel, Paul - *Fire Alarm!*, New Albany, IN, Squire Book Village, 1994
--------------- - "Theater of Death" *Firehouse Magazine*, December 1982

Editors of Country Beautiful - *Great Fires of America*, Waukesha, WI, Country Beautiful Corporation, 1973

Enright, Laura L. - *Chicago's Most Wanted*, Washington, D.C., Potomac Books, 2005

Everett, Marshall - *The Great Chicago Theater Disaster*, Chicago, IL, Publishers Union of America, 1904

Farr, Finis - *Chicago: A Personal History of America's Most American City*, New Rochelle, NY, Arlington House, 1973

Fields, Armond - *Eddie Foy: A Biography of a Great American Entertainer*, Jefferson, NC, McFarland, 1999

Flexner, Stuart and Doris - *The Pessimist's Guide to History*, New York, Quill, 2000

Fliege, Stu - *Tales and Trails of Illinois*, Urbana, IL, University of Illinois Press, 2002

Foy, Eddie and Calvin F. Harlow - *Clowning Through Life*, New York, NY, E.P. Dutton, 1928

Furtado, Peter - *The New Century 1900-1914*, London, Chancellor Press, 1993

Gelman, Woody and Barbara Jackson - *Disaster Illustrated*, New York, Harmony Books, 1976

Grossman, James R, Ann Durkin Keating, and Janice Reiff (editors) - *The Encyclopedia of Chicago*, Chicago, Il, University of Chicago Press, 2004

Hansen, Harry - *The Chicago*, New York, NY, Farrar and Rinehart, 1942

Harrison, Carter H. - *Growing Up with Chicago*, Chicago, IL, Ralph Fletcher Seymour Publisher, 1944
---------------------- - *Stormy Years*, New York, NY, Bobbs-Merril, 1935

Hayes, Dorsha B. - *Chicago: Crossroads of American Enterprise*, New York, NY, Julian Messner, Inc., 1944

Hoffer, Peter Charles - *Seven Fires: The Urban Infernos that Shaped America*, New York, NY, Public Affairs Group, 2006

Hogan, John F. and Alex A. Burkholder - *Forgotten Fires of Chicago*, Charleston, SC, History Press, 2014

Holland, Robert A. - *Chicago in Maps*, New York, NY, Rizzoli Books, 2005

Iroquois Theater History Website ffiiroquoistheater.comffl Ergoiamtoo, Inc., 2020

Kenlon, John - *Fires and Fire-fighters*, New York, NY, George H. Doran Company, 1913

Laurie, Joe, Jr. - *Vaudeville: From the Honky-Tonks to the Palace*, New York, NY, Henry Holt Publishers, 1953

Lindberg, Richard - *Return to the Scene of the Crime*, Nashville, TN, Cumberland House, 1999
---------------------- - *To Serve and Collect*, New York, NY, Praeger, 1991

Longstreet, Stephen - *Chicago: An Intimate Portrait of People, Pleasures, and Power 1860-1919*, New York, NY, David McKay Co., 1973

Lowe, David - *Chicago Interiors: Views of a Splendid World*, Chicago, IL, Contemporary Books, 1979

Lyons, Paul Roberts - *Fire in America*, Boston, MA, National Fire Protection Association, 1976

Mark, Norman - *Mayors, Madams, and Madmen*, Chicago, Il, Chicago Review Press, 1979

Masters, Edgar Lee - *The Tale of Chicago*, New York, NY, G.P. Putnam and Sons, 1933

McCurdy, D.B., Editor - *Lest We Forget: Chicago's Awful Theater Horror*, Chicago, IL, Memorial Publishing Company, 2004

Miller, Donald - *City of Century: The Epic of Chicago and the Making of America*, New Yor, NY, Simon and Schuster, 1996

Mirkin, Sanford - *When Did It Happen?*, New York, NY, Ives Washburn, 1957

Moreno, Richard - *It Happened in Illinois*, Guilford, CT, Globe-Pequot Press, 2011

Nash, Jay Robert - *Darkest Hours* - New York, NY, Simon and Schuster, 1976

Northrop, H.D. - *The World's Greatest Calamities*, 1904

Ogden, Tom, *Haunted Chicago*, Guilford, CT, Globe-Pequot Press, 2014

Paulett, John and Judy Floodstrand - *Lost Chicago*, London, Pavilion Books, 2021

Remer, Theodore - "Terror at the Iroquois" *Chicago Daily News*, December 30, 1967

Selzer, Adam - *Ghosts of Chicago*, Woodbury, MN, Llewellyn Publications, 2017
------------------ - *Mysterious Chicago*, New York, NY, Skyhorse Publishing, 2016

Smith, Henry Justin - *Chicago: A Portrait*, New York, NY, The Century Co., 1931

Steffens, Lincoln - *The Shame of the Cities*, American Century Series, New York, NY, Hill and Wang, 1957

Stranger, Wesley - *Rescued from a Fiery Death*, Chicago, IL, Laid and Lee Publishers, 1904

Swanston, Stevenson - *Chicago Days*, Chicago, IL, Chicago Tribune First Division Foundation, 1977

Taylor, Troy - *Haunted Chicago*, Alton, IL, Whitechapel Press, 2002
---------------- - *Murder and Mayhem in Downtown Chicago*, Charleston, SC, History Press, 2009

Taylor, Troy with Adam Selzer and Ken Melvoin-Berg, *Weird Chicago*, Chicago, IL, Whitechapel Press, 2009

Taylor, Troy and Rene Kruse - *And Hell Followed With it*, Chicago, IL, Whitechapel Press, 2010

Viskochil, Larry A. - *Chicago at the Turn of the Century in Photographs*, New York, NY. Dover, 1984

Weitzel, Tony - "Christmas Week 1903: Horror at the Iroquois Theatre" *Chicago Daily News*, December 28, 1963

Westerberg, Julia - "Looking Backward: The Iroquois Theater Fire of 1903," *Chicago History*, Winter 1978-1979

Billboard Magazine
Chicago Record-Herald
Chicago Tribune
Chicago Daily News
Chicago Post
Chicago Journal
Chicago Inter Ocean
Chicago American
Colliers Magazine
Fire and Engineering Magazine
Life Magazine
McClure's Magazine
New York Times
New York Herald
New York Sun

New York Post
New York Evening Journal
New York Telegram
Popular Mechanics Magazine
Reader's Digest
Smithsonian Magazine
Theater Magazine

Personal Interviews and Correspondence

SPECIAL THANKS TO:

April Slaughter: Cover Design and Artwork

Becky Ray: Editing and Proofreading

Lisa Taylor and Lux

Brianna Snow

Orrin and Rachel Taylor

Rene Kruse

Rachael Horath

Bethany Horath

Elyse and Thomas Reihner

John Winterbauer

Kaylan Schardan

Maggie and Packy Lundholm

Cody Beck

Tom and Michelle Bonadurer

Samantha Smith

Lydia Rhoades

Susan Kelly and Amy Bouyear

Cheryl Stamp and Sheryel Williams-Staab

Joelle Leitschuh and Tonya Leitschuh

And the entire crew of American Hauntings

ABOUT THE AUTHOR

Troy Taylor is the author of books on ghosts, hauntings, true crime, the unexplained, and the supernatural in America. He is also the founder of American Hauntings Ink, which offers books, ghost tours, events, and weekend excursions. He was born and raised in the Midwest and divides his time between Illinois and wherever the wind takes him.

See Troy's other titles at:
www.americanhauntingsink.com

CPSIA information can be obtained
at www.ICGtesting.com
Printed in the USA
LVHW051320181121
703543LV00002B/6

9 781735 270630